Editor: Rebecca Shivone Smith

All proceeds–and more–from the sale of this
book will go to the Guideposts Foundation

# Helping Hands

In the early stages of writing *The War Years* I needed the help of someone I knew… from correspondence only. It turned out to be Fred Lincoln (Brig. Gen. Retired) of the membership reunion, and Blue Devil Committees.

I had previous telephone conversations with Mr. Lincoln (usually with questions regarding my book — *The War Years* — and the use of photographs from *The Blue Devils in Italy* to illustrate the activities of the 88th Division in action. He had no objections and said "use what you need — no problem."

I am also grateful to Jonathan M. Gordon, partner of Alston & Bird, LLP, representing the Bill Mauldin Estate, LLC, for the use of Bill Mauldin illustrations in special situations.

And to Ms. Kathryn Stallard, Director of Special Collections and Archives at the Smith Library Center, Southwestern University.

# For the Record

**During World War II** there were 16,000,000 servicemen and women in uniform. By the year 2025 it has been estimated there will be less than 100,000 World War II veterans living.

Think about it.

From this large group. There are plenty of heroes to go around including Audie Murphy (from North Texas), my battalion commander Lt. Col. Charles P. Furr (from South Carolina), and Daniel Inouye, Hawaii, 442nd Regiment to mention just a few.

I never considered myself among this elite group.

I was never asked to volunteer for anything—nor did I "cut & run" from anything—nor consider doing so. When orders were given—I obeyed—and did my best to survive.

The same was true of my comrades. We were there for each other.

Years later on March 5, 2010 I hosted a dinner party for twenty guests.

During the evening, a friend requested that I share a particular wartime experience involving me and Company K, 88th Infantry Division in Volterra, Italy (I was surprised by this request but responded accordingly).

Upon completion, the wife of another friend had this to say "Raymond, you should write a book...*before 2025.*"

## Previous Books

First I wrote *The Journey*, then *The Gallery Years* (these two books are now combined into one book titled *The Journey to The Gallery Years*.

Followed by a special tribute to the French "Naif" painter Maurice Ghiglion-Green… in French and English with more than 50 illustrations in color.

Now is the time to share with you *The War Years*.

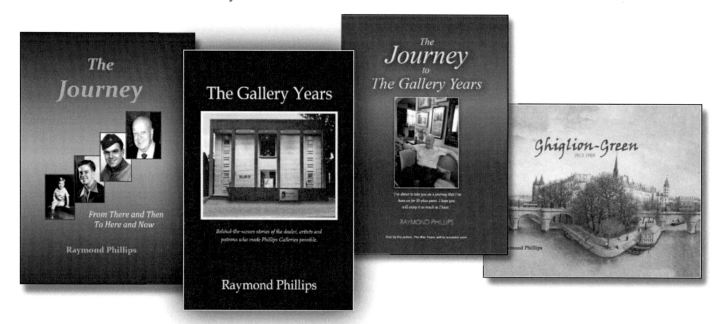

# Foreword

**I have been working** on a series of stories that have their origins with my first book *The Journey*. I found it to be a good "launching pad" for other books that would expand the original book with additional stories.

This proved to be true with *The Journey to the Gallery Years*, where additional artists and stories were presented in one complete manner.

*The War Years* (1941-1945) covers my experiences in World War II with much greater detail than before. Beginning slightly before Pearl Harbor and continuing to the end of the war.

Some of the stories are "repeats," all of them are true.

I came to understand that "whatever <u>could</u> happen" was not the same as "whatever <u>would</u> happen." You will also see what Divine Guidance and Divine Intervention can do.

## Personal Pledge

The net proceeds from the sale of this book will be contributed to the **Guideposts Foundation**.

*Raymond Phillips*

# CHAPTER 1

## The War Years, the beginning and before

On December 7, 1941, I was attending a high school fraternity meeting (Theta Kappa Omega or TKO). The meeting was being held in the home of fellow member, Perman Grundy. Also, attending the meeting were my friends, Dick Granbery, Billy Bob McLean, and Jack Saye.

Our meeting was interrupted by outside noise that grew louder by the minute.

When we went outside to investigate, the entire neighborhood had gathered to share the news coming from Pearl Harbor, Hawaii.

The Japanese were bombing Pearl Harbor and we knew that World War II had begun!

Raymond Phillips, Dick Granbery, Billy Bob McLean and Jack Saye

The next morning, in my typing class, our teacher began the session by reviewing the consequences of this terrible attack and saying, with tears, that every boy in the class would eventually be called to serve our country in this war.

Honolulu Star-Bulletin 1st EXTRA

6 PAGES—HONOLULU, TERRITORY OF HAWAII, U. S. A., SUNDAY, DECEMBER 7, 1941—6 PAGES     PRICE FIVE CENTS

# WAR !

(Associated Press by Transpacific Telephone)

SAN FRANCISCO, Dec. 7.— President Roosevelt announced this morning that Japanese planes had attacked Manila and Pearl Harbor.

# OAHU BOMBED BY JAPANESE PLANES

8

## Divine Guidance & Divine Intervention

**In my youth...** many years before I had heard of "Divine intervention..." I "felt" that a force—someone—or something would come to my rescue when I needed help. Just like in the old "Perils of Pauline" episodes at the movies on Saturday morning.

As "The War Years" unfold, you will be with me on many of these occasions. I promise you that—when they occur—and I report them, I am reporting the truth.

They always found me whenever I needed help.

Where did they come from?

A "heavenly" source—like from the sky above.

# The Day After Pearl Harbor

**On the night of December 8, 1941** and the nights that followed, I became aware of airplanes, flying over Marshall headed west. Marshall was not too far from Barksdale Field near Shreveport, Louisiana.

I couldn't help but think the planes were on their way to Japan to make the Japanese pay for the Pearl Harbor attack!

These nightly thoughts were consistent with the heroic news of Capt. Colin Kelly who bravely took on the enemy by bombing a Japanese cruiser and engaging the enemy in a very aggressive way. On the return to its base at Clark Field, a Japanese fighter attacked and severely damaged the American bomber. Kelly ordered his crew to bail out, but he was unable to exit the plane before it crashed. He was killed instantly.

As time went on, I continued the daily pace of Marshall High School and the High School band. On a very "hush-hush," secret basis our new band director, Fletcher Garner, selected the necessary orchestra members, ordered "stock arrangements" from a New York publisher and scheduled daily practice sessions, known only to the selected players.

We rehearsed in the band room located in an "out of the way area" not disturbing outsiders. It was our secret project.

Our rehearsals were daily, serious and wonderful!

At this point in time I was a subscriber to a wonderful publication named *Downbeat*. It's impossible for me to describe the joy of reading this monthly publication.

I read each edition again and again until the new edition arrived. The stories told gave me a "bird's eye view" of the Big Band world. I knew all of the players in all of the bands, and the itinerary of all orchestras and when members changed from one band to another, etc, etc.

This was the happiest time of my life so far.

Finally, it was time for the orchestra to go public! Our rehearsals were bringing us to our first public concert!

We had been "booked" to play to an audience of 300 to 400 in the school auditorium.

Quietly, we took our places on the stage behind closed curtains, the Master of Ceremony proudly announced as the curtains were opened the Premier exhibition of the MARSHALL HIGH SCHOOL ORCHESTRA!!!

The orchestra opened with "I FOUND MY THRILL ON BLUEBERRY HILL"—the audience went wild—and so did the orchestra.

We continued to increase our "repertoire" and began playing for high school dances!

As the war in Europe continued we were busy raising money for our English friends.

The orchestra played for the "Bundles for Britain" event on the terrace of the Hotel Marshall.

Marshall High School Dance Band under the direction of Fletcher Garner. This event was a "Bundles for Britain" fundraiser during WWII.

Pictured front row left to right: drums - Hugh Marshall; guitar - Richard Haynes; sax - Raymond Bostick, Donald Hendsley, Bobby Boyett, Tommy Dinwiddie.

Second row left to right: piano - A.W. Resser; Conductor - Fletcher Garner; trumpets - Sam Williams, Bill Merrill, Jack Saye; Trombones - Bill Graff, Raymond Phillips; bass - Carl Nowlin.

## Another Night to Remember

**Marshall was a dry** community, meaning that no alcoholic beverages could be sold publicly. This ruled out the appearances of bands like Glenn Miller, Harry James, Benny Goodman and others. *No booze = No jazz in Marshall!* However, about 25-30 miles west of Marshall, the world was different, and the Big Bands could perform in nightclubs as they traveled between the east and west coast at places like Mattie Castleberry's "Palm Isle." And that's exactly where Tommy Dorsey's orchestra was engaged to play on the evening of March 16, 1942.

The Tommy Dorsey Orchestra was my favorite.

*Tommy Dorsey*

I could hardly control myself. I wanted to be fully prepared for the evening of my life. I typed a format of the Dorsey orchestra personnel, section by section, in order to get autographs of all the band members, including the leader Dorsey.

As the players appeared on the bandstand in preparation for the performance, I carefully observed them one at a time. I wanted to select a player who looked "receptive" to start the process of signing and passing the format along—section by section—to the other band members.

Henry Beau, in the sax section, was selected to start the process.

GETTING SENTIMENTAL WITH

Tommy Dorsey

WHO?
MARIE
STAR DUST
SONG OF INDIA
LITTLE WHITE LIES
ROYAL GARDEN BLUES
I'LL NEVER SMILE AGAIN
I'M GETTIN' SENTIMENTAL OVER YOU

VICTOR RECORDS

A VOLUME OF HIS FAMOUS HITS

Everything was going great until the format was passed to Buddy Rich, a truly great drummer with an unpredictable personality. He wasn't interested in signing until Frank Sinatra came to the rescue by saying, "Give the kid a break!"

And, he did!

The final signature belonged to Tommy Dorsey himself. It completed the process... *or so I thought* — the signature of Connie Haines came later... March 20, 2004 as reported on page 17. I was so overwhelmed by having obtained all these signatures that when I got home at 3 a.m. I just had to pull out the trombone and play like Dorsey! I was so inspired!

In charged my dad. He was furious at my having awakened him and probably the whole neighborhood.

*Tommy Dorsey Orchestra. This is virtually the same orchestra used on the recording cover on page 50. Some notables: (back row) Jo Stafford (black dress), Connie Haines (white dress) and Frank Sinatra (next to Connie and behind drummer, Buddy Rich). Ziggy Elman on trumpet right in front of Jo. Freddie Stulce on front row, third from left. Joey Bushkin on piano and Tommy Dorsey standing next to piano.*

TOMMY DORSEY & HIS ORCHESTRA
****

I. Saxes:

II. Trumpets:

III. Trombones:

IV. Drums:

V. Piano:

VI. Bass:

VII. Guitar:

VIII. Vocalists:

_Tommy Dorsey, Leader_

---

*Raymond A. Phillips*
*4629 Mockingbird Lane*
*Dallas, TX 75209*

March 20, 2002

Ms. Connie Haines
c/o Mrs. Seymour Heller
520 North Camden Drive
Beverly Hills, CA 90210

Dear Ms. Haines:

On March 16, 1942, I traveled with four high school friends to neighboring Longview, Texas to hear the Tommy Dorsey Orchestra perform a one night engagement.

At this time, I played the trombone in the Marshall, Texas High School dance orchestra. You can imagine what Tommy Dorsey meant to me.

In my high school typing class I prepared a format that could be circulated among the musicians in hopes of getting all of their autographs.

This was a momentous occasion and I went prepared to make the most of it.

It worked- and the autographs were placed inside a Tommy Dorsey album when I went into World War II service in 1943.

Many years later- (circa 1998-1999) - the Longview Public Library found, in their archives, a copy of the 1942 newspaper advertisement of this event and sent it to me.

The advertisement revealed that my efforts had not been entirely successful. Indeed, there was a very important omission - the autograph of Connie Haines!

I hope its not too late to correct this oversight.

Would you kindly provide me with your autograph after these 60 years?

Thank you, in advance, for your consideration and contribution to this memorial.

Yours very truly,

Raymond A. Phillips

Enclosures

THE SENTIMENTAL GENTLEMAN

**TOMMY DORSEY**

AND HIS ORCHESTRA featuring FRANK SINATRA
BUDDY RICH · ZIGGY ELMAN · CONNIE HAINES
AND THE PIED PIPERS · ALL IN PERSON!

MONDAY
**MARCH 16**

# PALM ISLE CLUB

NINE 'TIL 2 A. M.—ADVANCE, 1.50 PER PERSON

Advance Tickets and Table Reservations on Sale at:
Etex Cafe, Longview ● Blackstone Cafe, Kilgore
Bill's Confectionery, Gladewater

To Raymond ~
Please add my autograph to your
collection ~ God Bless!
Connie Haines

P.S. I tho't you'd never ask (Ha) 60 yrs later

*Connie Haines*

# CHAPTER 2

## There's No Place Like Home... my family before the war

**D**aily, my mother and dad were up no later than 6:00 a.m., visiting in the kitchen... alone... after their breakfast while they talked. Mom was busy preparing dad's lunch. Dad always started his workday at 7:00 a.m. He took his lunch to the T&P railroad shops where he worked as a blacksmith or boilermaker... whichever was needed at the time. Dad was rather short in height, well under six feet, and extraordinarily strong.

One would be foolish to "take on" my dad. He was, by nature, always kind and considerate of others. However, he was not to be engaged in an aggressive manner.

My mom was indefatigable. Raising three boys and one girl, without domestic help... except for Ernestine, who was "missing" an arm but this did nothing to slow the load of washing with my mother. All bed clothes for two weeks plus everything washable, was put in this giant iron container, full of boiling water (from a wood burning fire)

in our backyard. After a thorough washing, all items were hung on the outside clothesline for nature to dry.

Life during the Great Depression (1929-1941) was no picnic.

My mother's father, Abraham Bradburn, came to America from England in the late 1800s at the urging of an older brother, a civil engineer employed by the Union Pacific railroad, building the rail lines to the far west. My grandfather was trained to minister the gospel in the Methodist church in Victorian England. He earned his income as a cabinet man in the cars department of the T&P railroad. He came to live with us after the death of my grandmother, whom I never knew. My grandfather worked for the railroad during the week. On Sunday he preached in the rural areas of Harrison County, for which he was paid with a home-cooked meal in the home of a member of the congregation.

Boy, he could really eat.

Once, I went with him in his Model-T Ford to have lunch in the home of a farm family. Their dining table was created by a pair of "carpenter-horses" that supported a wooden panel serving as the table top… it was covered with a very inviting "oil cloth panel" in forest green. The end result could have been the cover of *House and Garden* magazine…

However, its treasure was discovered with the meal put before us.

Although he was very slim in stature, grandfather had the appetite of two hungry men.

Our hostess just "beamed" in culinary triumph as my grandfather ate with unrivaled enthusiasm.

# Divine Guidance Returns to Music

**School was over** for the year. I was on the front porch, visiting with my mother. Mom was "shelling peas" when the phone rang. Her conversation was brief. Mr. Tom Johnson was calling to see if it would be convenient to come by for a visit.

Mr. Johnson was the band director at Southwestern University in Georgetown, Texas, and was on a recruiting mission. He had been visiting with the Marshall High School band director when asked if he could recommend any band members who could play to the standards required by Southwestern University. My director gave him my name and telephone number.

When Mr. Johnson arrived he requested that I play something on my trombone… anything… exercises… songs… and so I played "Georgia on My Mind," from the living room, while he and my mom sat nearby on the front porch.

*Tom Johnson*

I played a few exercises in "warming up" and a few improvisations just to "show off."

He then asked me to return to the porch for more conversation.

Mr. Johnson was authorized to offer a scholarship that covered everything: tuition, books, room and board, everything required if I would come to Southwestern University and play in the band. WOW!

There was however, one requirement: service in the dining room in the girl's dormitory… waiting on two tables of eight girls each.

# Georgetown—Here We Come

**The day of departure arrived**. My mother and dad—plus brother Elgin—packed my belongings and off we went in search of Georgetown.

It was southwest of Marshall, below Waco, slightly above Austin, in central Texas.

The closer we got to our destination, the quieter we became (that in itself was a major event for the Phillips family).

We finally found Georgetown, Southwestern University was very near the town center. Finding Mood Hall came next.

As we came closer—we all grew quieter.

This was the first time for "good byes" and I wasn't sure the "scholarship" was worth this price.

As my family finally departed for the return to Marshall, I discovered "homesickness" for the first time. Unfortunately, I would not go home until Thanksgiving.

(When I returned to Southwestern University after being home for the holiday I was never "homesick" again.)

PS: This condition was a great "plus" for me during the war years. Many of the GI's had never been away from home and they really felt the "homesickness" and Uncle Sam made "zero" allowance for this condition.

# Southwestern University Reunion via the 1943 Yearbook

**Tom Johnson was** an important part of my life during the post high school years and the early years in the military. I could not believe a photograph of Tom Johnson would be hard to find. The internet acknowledged Southwestern University but did not have "Tom Johnson." Several phone calls put me in touch with the librarian Ms. Kathryn Stallard, Director, Special Collections and Archives, Smith Library Center, who maintains the control and integrity of what was needed to make the reader aware of this "jewel institution," Southwestern University. Beginning with a picture of Mood Hall (from the Southwestern University special collections) that was built circa 1908.

Mood Hall was a special accommodation at the time. I shared the largest room with Bill Holmes and Max Stanaland… both band members.

I was a freshman living with a junior and a senior.

We had a ball.

Also, among the yearbook photos, were the university concert and dance band (if you are still interested, you will see me playing the trombone and room-mate Bill Holmes on the drums). And I am pleased to report that I finally have a Tom Johnson photo. In fact, I have two, one as the Southwestern recruiter at my home in Marshall, circa 1941, and photo #2 after he became an Army band leader… and continued his effort to have me transferred to his Army band at Camp Hulen on the Gulf Coast. Tom was not one to give up. He tried to get me transferred from Camp Wolters, Camp Fannin, Ft. Meade, and Camp Patrick Henry and continued the effort all the way to the Infantry Replacement Centers in Italy!

*Southwestern University, Administration Building*

*Southwestern University, Mood Hall*

# Strike Up the Band

**The Southwestern University band** was very unusual. It was composed of "zero" extra players. There were never two or more players for each part (for example, the University of Texas band could have 15 or 20 trombone players performing and arrangements that required only 2 or 3 trombone players). Southwestern had two.

The Southwestern band did not march and play on the field at halftime! Instead, it performed a concert facing the stadium… with special arrangements created by an outstanding alto sax player from Port Arthur named Ray Davidson.

No traditional marches (sorry Mr. Sousa), we primarily played big band music.

Southwestern University was the oldest college in Texas. It was founded in 1840. It never aspired to be the largest. In fact the enrollment was limited to about 450 students at the time of my entrance (I have learned that the current enrollment is about 1350 students).

(During WWII Southwestern University had a V-12 U.S. Navy training program that changed the campus life as I experienced it.)

## "In the Mood" with Max and Bill

**When I moved into Mood Hall**, I met the two band members who would be my roommates. One was a minister's son who had transferred to Southwestern from the University of Texas in Austin.

His name was Bill Holmes, former member of the UT fencing team. He was handsome, spirited, and had a way with girls. Bill was also a spirited drummer, *a la* Gene Krupa. Bill was good looking and all of the aforementioned; he was another "Errol Flynn" sent over to Mood Hall by Central Casting.

One Sunday morning our door opened and this solemn, serious man came in without being asked. Bill Holmes broke the silence by exclaiming, "hello dad, what a surprise."

The response was, "get dressed, we are going to see the Dean." The look on Bill's face said it all… *Doomsville*.

During the meeting with the Dean, Bill's dad announced his intention of removing Bill from school and bringing him home. He was not satisfied with the grading reports that had revealed an unsatisfactory record on every subject.

The Dean had this to say: "if your son would complete his assignments he would receive 'high marks'. As it stands, his record is not 'low,' it is 'incomplete.'"

Bill's father said, "Bill, your mother and I want you to live up to everything you were taught and get serious with your studies… or else!"

Raymond Phillips

Bill Holmes

26

## Max Stanaland

**There is only one Max**—anywhere—he was from Tyler and his mom, a widow, lived in a small garage apartment. Max was the opposite of "wild" Bill.

The local dry cleaner in Georgetown hired Max to represent them.

Male students would bring their clothes to Max—who would turn them over to the cleaner—to clean and re-deliver to Mood Hall.

He was such a kind soul and would have difficulty dealing with students who were less than prompt in paying for this service.

After the war years, recounting the past with my friend Chuck Mandernach—I mentioned the name "Max Stanaland." Chuck not only knew Max but had played "jobs" together in Dallas.

Chuck helped get the telephone number in Tyler where Max lived. I could hardly wait to call him. The phone rang several times before a lady answered. When I asked to speak with Max there was a long pause, "Are you a friend of Max?"

There was something about that question—or the hesitant manner—that made me feel something was terribly wrong.

Max had gone to heaven… one day before my call.

## Scatter Shooting at Southwestern

**Being the largest dormitory** room in Mood Hall ours seemed to attract the largest "bull-shooters." We were located on the second floor, directly above the apartment of coach Randolph Medley, sports director and the target of "hardwood noise"… created by lifting a wooden side-chair… and dropping it to the hardwood floor resulting in a resounding, hopefully disturbing noise.

If he were at home, this would get the attention of coach Medley… known to these reckless noise makers as "muscle head Medley."

(For the record: Coach Medley was not and did not deserve the name "muscle head.")

**As we gathered daily,** in our room in Mood Hall, one could hear the sound of cowboy boots, en route to our session—none other than "Mr. Know it All." The son of a Methodist minister from Beaumont, prize student of Dr. George Hester, head of the Government and History department, the one and only Mr. John Tower. He was welcomed to our daily discussions of world affairs—and beautiful women.

As a future US Senator, he had an opinion on all things known to man. He also played French horn in the band… somewhat.

# Rooftop Tradition

**Southwestern was founded** in 1840 — a long held tradition existed at Mood Hall — being the oldest university in Texas. It went like this:

A volunteer freshman would be responsible for "painting his class number on the standing-seam, metal roof." In my case, the class number would be #43 applied undetected during the night.

If caught in the act of painting each upperclassman could "apply 43 paddle slaps across your posterior"

My upper class room-mates felt that I should see this tradition sustained as an honor for "our room."

Really?

I carefully gathered the necessary supplies — a bucket of paint, a sturdy brush, a ladder to help me climb to the chosen location — very near class #42. The weather was in my favor and the silent strokes, applied with masterful intent, made me feel confident in attaining the required result.

This was a "solo" event — with no "triumphant" sharing… with anyone.

Regretfully, there was "no triumph."

At breakfast, the following day the "table talk" raised some questions about this effort and who should be held "accountable."

I listened to the upper class snide remarks with my "paint-scarred" hands under the table — out of sight.

The only benefit for me — I was not caught in the act and they were denied the paddle.

# The Many Moods of Mac

One of my closest friends at Southwestern was McLaurin Meredith. "Mac" was a ministerial major and one of the most cheerful souls in the kitchen at Laura Kykendall Hall.

While others waited tables Mac preferred the huge dish-washing process, with great energy and spirit, stripped to the waist, he was in his element.

We shared this activity daily. Mac also shared a strongly held belief in achieving and sustaining physical fitness.

It should be noticed that he was a very good example of physical fitness: over six feet in height, very trim waist, large, muscular shoulders and arms. Another Charles Atlas.

Mac confided in me the following theory:

"If you lift" a new born calf, <u>every day</u>, and continue the procedure, daily, you will be able to lift <u>from calf to cow</u>. No problem.

Think about this.

This theory was also applied to the weather.

If you went swimming in the nearby San Gabriel river <u>every day</u>—without fail—one could enjoy the swim all year long regardless of the weather.

Eager to experience this, I accepted his invitation. Daily, we went to a choice location in the San Gabriel, a curved location, among the rocks on three sides… almost a natural, private pool.

This experience of daily weather has a lot in common with daily weight. September-October, come and gone, no problems, so far.

However, early November produced a "blue norther" that almost made an "ice rink" on the San Gabriel—as to the"McLaurin-Meredith theory," I had only this to say to my friend Mac: "Your calf became a full grown cow… overnight!"

"Lets go back to Mood Hall and get warm."

**Thumbs Up**

These were the days of "hitch-hiking." One could go to Austin, some thirty miles away just by putting a thumb in the air—wait—and "bingo," a Good Samaritan stopped to pick up three happy travelers.

Bill Holmes was so particular that he would inquire, "Do you have a radio?" If not, he would refuse the "free" ride and wait for the music man (or woman) to stop and give us a ride.

Max and I also went along for the ride with Bill—only if there were a radio in the car.

**I found a hidden treasure in a Biology class.**

There truly was more going on at Southwestern than the daily Mood Hall "bull sessions."

I had never been one to study courses in the world of science; Chemistry, Physics, Biology were strangers to me.

At Southwestern, science was a required elective on my degree plan. The sooner I could attend to this obligation the better. I registered for an introduction to Biology 101… in the Science Hall

As I remember it, the Science Hall could have been a concert hall.

Student seating began with the "top" row — near the ceiling. Additional seating rows declined in a disciplined manner down to a lower level from which Dr. Gordon Wolcott conducted his teaching. It reminded me of a concert hall — where everyone could observe the maestro — and he them — in full view.

Dr. Wolcott was a dedicated teacher. He made his subject very appealing and understandable.

It was my last exposure to this field of study and it was well worth the time.

# When it Rains — it Pours

**The Southwestern Dance Band** rarely played for dances "off campus." First of all, we did not have a band bus and lack of transportation put a limit on our availability.

That came to an end when an offer came to travel to Camp Hood (now known as Fort Hood ) near Lampasas. We really needed several cars to accommodate our needs. We had to "borrow" two or three.

Thelma Bradshaw — a friend from Grapeland — was dating a student who had a five passenger Ford.

He was persuaded to loan the Ford, however, he made a point of its limitation.

If the brakes were applied suddenly — the car headlights would fail. To be safe — we carried a supply of fuses in the glove compartment.

With the transportation issue solved, we left for the dance job.

During the evening, the weather changed from slight rain to heavy rain. After the dance was over, we gathered our instruments and headed for Georgetown… in a downpour.

As we approached Lampasas, we noticed that the town policeman was making the rounds, checking the doors of stores to make sure that everything was secure.

In addition to his "side arm" he carried a flashlight — with which he signaled for us to stop… here and now.

Our driver obeyed so suddenly that our car headlights turned off... just as we had been warned.

The police officer was really concerned about this unexpected situation... but relaxed when we informed him of our remedy.

We quickly replaced the fuses and the lights went on again—and so did we.

At last, we were on our way back to Georgetown—and the Southwestern campus—when the car stopped again. This time it was not a fuse problem.

We had run out of gasoline!

The magic of Bill Holmes "hitch-hiking" was not very good at this hour of the day. So, we started walking.

Our bass player, Franklin Pickle, was from Georgetown and his father was in the Williamson County Police Department. Pickle made the suggestion that we could avoid the embarrassment of the late hour, on the road, carrying musical instruments by going to the county jail where there were some vacant cells for us to use until later in the morning.

All memories should have a happy ending—like this one.

# A Rare Musical Moment

**Among the various teachers** that I remember, was Professor Henry Meyer, dean of the School of Fine Arts.

As professor of piano and organ he introduced me to the wide world of classical music. He made sure that Mozart, Beethoven, Bach, and Brahms received proper recognition.

From time to time, he would illustrate distinctions in their music on the piano.

During the course I found myself thinking of the future—and a career in music.

Would it bring a happy, rewarding life?

I concluded that it would.

That being the case, I should prepare myself for the future and transfer to North Texas State Teachers College in Denton.

This inclusion added a lot to the course and I must say that I received more from Professor Meyer than anyone else in the class. That is the whole truth—because—I was the <u>only student</u> in the class.

(I was also aware of time marching on and I would soon be age 18. Uncle Sam would be looking for me if the war in North Africa & the Pacific was still in need of servicemen.)

# CHAPTER 3

## Good-bye Georgetown, Hello Denton

Sadly, it was time to say "good bye" to Southwestern University. It was—and is—a great school.

The valuable scholarship that made Southwestern affordable for me was no longer required.

The Denton campus and student body were much larger—into the thousands compared to the hundreds at Southwestern.

Male students were becoming fewer in number. World War II was taking the male students as they turned 18 years of age.

On June 6, I would become a member of this group.

One must pass an audition by the school director, Dr. Wilfred C. Bain. After passing the test, I was now ready to study and make music—plus some needed "walking around money." These two items were solved by playing in the stage show band every Saturday night… in the school auditorium.

A stage show would be followed by a movie.

The stage show was created and directed by Floyd Graham—widely known as "Fessor Graham," a one of a kind maestro.

And the program was strictly "big band music," enhanced by dancers, vocalists, etc. It was a very professional training experience.

This event was also rewarding in the money department. Each musician made $1.50 every Saturday night!

On Wednesday night an outdoor tennis or basketball "slab" was used for dancing… and… we each made another $1.50 tax free.

Wow!

My room was in a new dormitory on the top floor of the music hall. Each room would accommodate two male students, $25.00 per month, total.

I took my meals in one of the several boarding houses surrounding the campus.

Mrs. Hopkins was the owner/operator of my choice. Her dining service was considered the best in town.

During this period, a good friend from Marshall High School days had just completed high school but was not going to college. He was from a very poor family and there was no money for college. I really went to work on him to get him to come to Denton.

We would share the $25 room rent at $12.50 each, per month.

He would earn $3.00 per week in the stage show and "slab" bands, etc. This covered most of the money needs, the rest would find a way. His name was Raymond Bostick, age 16 and went on to become very popular on the campus and a successful high school band director after college.

I was the "Raymond" who would turn 18 on June 6, 1943 and received a letter from Uncle Sam—"come join us in *The War Years.*"

(Just for the record: Tom Johnson, my mentor at Southwestern, joined the Army as a band director at Camp Hulen, Palacios, Texas and wanted me transferred to his band… when I was inducted into the Army.)

This is the opening "salvo "of a long series of transfer requests that followed me from basic training to a foxhole.

My friend, ministerial student at Southwestern, Don Box, had been calling me "Foxhole Phillips" for some time.

Somehow—he predicted my future address.

## The War Years

At this moment in the journey, I am taking pause — the Army had a special way of taking pause. The squad or platoon leader gave the order to stop, followed by "smoke, if you've got 'em."

I was drafted, "by friends and neighbors" as the local draft board expressed it… to start the process of military service. Not an invitation, no "Would you consider?" They wanted me.

So desperately — on October 2, 1943 — that they provided free transportation from Marshall, Texas to Mineral Wells, Texas — the location of Camp Wolters. (By the way, this was the procedure all regional draftees or enlistees experienced… including a young Texan from Hunt County-in North Texas... who also came into the Army at Camp Wolters and was almost "rejected" for being "under weight" at 121 pounds. He went on to serve in the most meritorious way. His name was Audie Murphy. "There was no comparison between Audie & me — I weighed 165 pounds.")

# CHAPTER 4

## To Director Tom Johnson: be advised, I am on my way

**T**he bus ride to the induction station in Tyler was uneventful. I did not know another person on board, so this gave me time to think about my destination. Tom Johnson had been commissioned the new band director at Camp Hulen in Palacios, Texas and he requested that I notify him at the time of my induction and he would put in a transfer request with the Army at Camp Wolters, Texas, for me to be transferred to Camp Hulen. He wanted to create a new band at Camp Hulen with former members of the Southwestern University band.

Tom was quite the operator and I was really fortunate to have him on my side.

On we went to Mineral Wells, Texas and the beginnings of a new adventure. One would never suspect me of being on the edge of enlistment. I was attired in my timely musician outfit. Pseudo "zoot slacks," but far from the customary high-waisted, slim tapered to just above the ankles in order to fully reveal those great loafers, a haircut barely acceptable to my dad.

Uncle Sam was about to receive an unusual recruit.

Man, I was really "hip."

After responding to a roll call confirming my arrival, we headed for another location. We were ordered to undress, hang-up our clothes and get ready for a physical exam—Army style.

I found this to be just another routine experience until I tried hanging-up my trousers.

Where was my wallet? In my whole life, never would I mention this to my mother, who had the "crazy notion" that I would lose the wallet if I kept it in my back pocket.

I reported this loss to my new commanders and they advised me to telephone the bus station and report my loss <u>after</u> they had completed their paper work.

I thought this was a hopeless suggestion but when you have no other idea, you go with it.

As suggested, I made the call and guess what? My wallet had been discovered.

I did not recognize the true nature of this event at the time. It came to me—as unexpectedly as the college scholarship.

It arrived just when needed.

# All Goes Well at Mineral Wells — Ultimately

**The wallet discovery came when** the bus interior was being cleaned.

I am forever grateful for this discovery and keeping the contents from falling into the wrong hands. I am especially thankful that they didn't call my mother, whose name, address and phone number were also inside my wallet.

Now we were assigned a barracks with bunk beds and still had the custody of our own clothing until GI clothes could be issued (I could hardly wait.)

Very early the next morning while still dark, a "loud mouth" corporal entered our barracks with the most unfortunate voice, ordering in triple fortissimo "let go of your ____," *(it rhymes with clocks)* "and grab your socks." "You are not home anymore!" (Really?)

We were ordered to go outside and line up for roll-call.

Quite honestly, I would have gladly gone home for breakfast but that was not allowed.

I realized that I was now Pvt. Raymond A. Phillips… 38480528. There was no comfort knowing no one else had the same number.

Nor was it any comfort in removing my civilian clothes and placing them in a bag (provided by the Army) pre-paid to my home in Marshall… another moment for my mother to deal with.

# Getting Acquainted with "All" Forms of Our New Life

**After many hours of questions** and forms were completed we finally arrive at the most explicit orientation on a subject rarely discussed: "venereal disease."

I must admit that I had heard of the varieties but had never before been exposed to such alarming presentations complete with photographs of the numerous examples of V.D., how they are acquired and you are convinced that no one can survive this type of infection.

At age 18 I was ready to quit dating forever.

Finally, we had survived the welcoming and were now curious about our destinations.

It had always been assumed that the draftee would be assigned to some distant Army post far from home so the individual GI would learn to cope with "home sickness."

That is why I was sure to be sent to a northeast location, such as NYC, and spend my weekends listening to the likes of the Dorsey's, Artie Shaw and other big bands and enjoying the northeast for the first time.

At the end of the day, it didn't matter. The anticipated Tom Johnson transfer would direct me to Camp Hulen at Palacios, Texas… as expected.

Now we were ready to go through all kinds of testing and general orientation of some of the realities of Army life. We had tests to determine IQ… whether we could read or write, etc.

I was surprised to learn that many of the new recruits were illiterate.

They were put in special classes at the camp to teach them the basics of reading and writing.

*Camp Wolters. Courtesy: Boyce Ditto Public Library, Mineral Wells, Texas.*

# Verdict

**In a closed envelope,** I opened to discover that I would be assigned to Camp Fannin, Texas.

Never heard of it.

Well, it is between Tyler and Gladewater, Texas.

It turned out that Fannin was a new U.S. Army training center. Or to put it more precisely U.S. Army Infantry Replacement Training Center. It was here that I met Chester H. Bowen who has a story of his own, but since Chet is no longer with us, I will make you better acquainted with him as we go along.

*Camp Fannin, Texas, 1944. Source: campfannin.net*

# Camp Fannin, Texas

**On one of the first days in Camp Fannin,** we came to realize that we were not alone. We were gathered as a group responding to the morning roll call when our attention quickly changed to a large platoon of soldiers marching in perfect unison.

The marchers were really putting on a show. Instead of rifles, they carried shovels!

They wore uniforms that were different from ours. They also had soft caps, somewhat like ours. Caps pretty much on the order of ours except for the color. They were in uniforms, very much in style and color that matched those I had seen in newsreels of the German soldiers, captured in North Africa… blue-gray.

Our sergeant informed us to take notice of these marchers for they were what we would be "up against" should we be sent to Italy.

These were German prisoners of war who were captured during the campaign in North Africa!

I had no idea that German POW's existed at Camp Fannin.

In fact, I didn't even know that Camp Fannin existed.

It had not existed as a training center very long. In fact, we would be the first GI's to receive basic training at Fannin. The camp was still under construction and the barracks we occupied were the first available.

(The German POWs had other accommodations.)

I quickly learned the daily demands for maintaining order and neatness. As in everything in the Army, our beds required a very high level of "neatness." There was a right way—the Army way—and it must be observed!

The sheet and blanket cover had to pass a very strenuous test every morning. The daily inspection was made to see if we—the newcomers—had prepared our beds and a tidy footlocker in the only acceptable way. The US Army way.

The bed clothes must be so tight that "flipping a quarter" in the air above the bed would "bounce" on landing.

Try it sometime.

The inspector had to be satisfied with the manner in which our barrack was maintained and the failure of just one bed or footlocker out of the group would result in group punishment of a wide variety.

(You could not avoid remembering that your "friends and neighbors" letter of draft notice had made this change and you would like to reciprocate.)

I was introduced to a whole new world—just men. All shapes and sizes, speaking different forms of the English language from the many different parts of the country.

There were boys from Virginia who sounded like they were from England.

There were two from New Orleans that no one could understand, and there were two from Oklahoma who did not speak at all.

They were from the Indian world and, so help me, one was "Private Barefoot" and the other "Private Rainwater."

When a complaint was made to the sergeant that one among us needed a bath, he reminded us that we would be judged as individuals but punished as a group.

As a group, we carried the offender bodily to the small shower building and scrubbed him thoroughly, in spite of the loud protests with vows of retribution.

As it turned out, he slowly, but surely, recovered from the embarrassment and became acceptable and clean.

My relationship with Chet Bowen grew into a level of friendship that saved the day in spite of the age difference of roughly ten years.

Tom Johnson continued to make transfer requests without success. The latest response informed him that the new policy—transfers could not be made until the soldier had completed his basic training of 16 weeks—made it clear that, before becoming a bandsman I would be an Infantry Replacement trainee and Camp Fannin for this kind of training.

They introduced us to the M-1 rifle and the rifle range. I learned how to use, clean, and carry this weapon of power. It weighed about 9-10 lbs. and had a clip of eight cartridges. I had no trouble passing the test but really preferred the lighter carbine about half the weight. My scores on the range were much higher with the carbine.

As basic training continued I could sense that a career in the Army was out of the question. Playing the trombone was more to my liking but you go where you are assigned and Tom Johnson was trying. I realized that I should forget the transfer and "go with the flow."

After about twelve or more weeks of infantry training that included a brief orientation with a gas mask in and out of an enclosure where gas was introduced plus learning how to crawl under bob-wire while <u>live ammo</u> was fired above your head. Also, the use of a bayonet was barely included, not that I cherished the possibility of that happening, but I had seen too many movies from Hollywood to be unaware of this weapon.

Trainees enter the gas chamber to test masks.

On reflection, I was persuaded that the urgent need for infantry replacements was great, North Africa, Sicily and Italy had been very costly.

These were really "crash programs" not equal to training at the Ranger level. But we were close to our 16 weeks and had one more week to experience living away from the barracks. It was called "bivouac."

We lived and continued training in a remote area of the camp in "pyramidal tents" that could accommodate 6-8 soldiers per tent.

We were introduced to C-rations of different varieties. Before you could adjust to this another treat was presented. This was known as K-ration. It came in three different flavors, each in a box, similar in size to the familiar *Cracker Jack* box. The three choices were B-L-S (breakfast-lunch-supper), mid-night snacks were not included.

Having grown-up in east Texas, Marshall, I was accustomed to <u>red soil</u> that produced good quality red bricks. Some of Camp Fannin was like this but the sand at the bivouac area was white like a beach. I was not familiar with this color and being the only Texan in our platoon, I could not explain this soil change to myself, let alone guys from other states.

Finally, our week of bivouac was over and we would be given a weekend pass. As soon as we returned to the barracks, all made a dash to the camp barber shop for a real professional shave.

This photo, taken in 1943, constitutes about a third of the men who had gone through the basic training process at Camp Fannin. After 16 weeks, our picture was taken. We subsequently got our orders to go to different destinations, mine being Fort Ord, California. Within minutes, the orders were changed sending me to Ft. Meade, Maryland. Divine intervention was in play!

The arrow on the left points to me. The one on the right points to Chet Bowen.

Since I was only 18, I was not in need of much of a shave. Rather than wait in the long line ahead of me I came up with a great idea I had observed at home. My father and grandfather used a razor unlike the one being used in the camp barber shop. Instead of getting in line, I asked the barber if I could shave myself using his "straight edge razor."

I will never forget his reply, "Go ahead, if you know how to use this type of razor."

"What's to know?" I was soon to learn that it would have been better had I not gotten a shave at all, just gone to Gladewater 15 miles away and used the razor of my brother-in-law. Well, all I can say is that haste makes a lot more than waste. It makes a bloody mess that requires a record number of "paper-patches" all over the face.

So, basic training was over and upon the return from the weekend pass, we will be told what the next assignment would be.

My hope is I will be assigned to a post near New York near the locations where the big bands play, like I had read about in the *Downbeat* magazine. I could hardly wait.

"Name" bands were often on the movie theater programs… such as the Paramount Theater.

*The Paramount Theatre, New York, New York*

# Basic Training is Over—for Now

**Now that our basic training was over**, the next move was in the hands of the U.S. Army. Surely, this would be the moment Tom Johnson's transfer request for my transfer to Camp Hulen would be honored and I would start playing the trombone again.

All of the GI's were assembled in a large recreation hall for the purpose of receiving orders where to report next for duty.

This was referred to as the "where and when" because the Army was so considerate (ha). They allowed a week to ten days *delay en route* for the GI—or soldier—to spend extra family time before going overseas.

I still clung to the notion that if the Tom Johnson transfer request did not pass the test then I would be assigned a post somewhere in the New York area. That would make it easy to hear in person both Dorsey's, Harry James, Benny Goodman, Count Basie, Charlie Barnett, the list is endless.

Well, when my name was called to come to the front desk and pick up the envelope containing my order—for my eyes only—it was not what I expected. (We were also ordered to remain in the hall until each order had been issued.)

The envelopes containing the orders also contained train tickets, one way to your destination. My order was for me to report to Ft. Ord, California!

Well, the big band dream was not to be.

It made no reference to the Tom Johnson transfer request, instead I was headed the wrong way… Fort Ord, California!

Fort Ord, California was the usual departure site for GI's going to the Pacific Theatre. However, if you were assigned to Fort Meade, Maryland you would be going to the Mediterranean theatre.

I spent a good deal of time thinking about the big bands in California. Los Angeles would probably have something to offer… probably.

While I gave this unexpected destination some serious thought I was interrupted by an announcement on the address system, "the following soldiers…" mentioned by their Army serial numbers were ordered to come forward with their original orders!

"Private 38480528 come forward."

My response was immediate. I was ordered to surrender the original order. When this was given to the officer in charge, he gave me another envelope containing an order to report to Ft. Meade, Maryland.

DIVINE GUIDANCE had other plans.

## On My Way to—Wherever

**I had ten days** as *delay en route*. I spent some time in Gladewater with my sister and the rest in Marshall with my parents. Most, if not all, my friends were in the service—scattered all over the world—my brothers were in service overseas, so it was not a reunion.

The day came for me to use my train ticket to Ft. Meade, Maryland.

Mom drove me to the train station… my dad was working at the T&P shops… it was just me and mom… to say farewell. We really did not say much. The moments were quiet but she always wanted me to be sure to check my pocket and keep my wallet safe.

All of the right words would come to me later… but I knew in my heart of hearts that we both would worry about each other.

As the train headed north… on its way to St. Louis… I realized that this was my first trip north of Marshall, Texas. As a newsboy, selling papers at the train station, I remembered selling to people headed all directions. Marshall was a "hub" for trains going south to New Orleans or west to Dallas and Fort Worth. This was my maiden voyage north of Marshall, Texas! What a trip!

The train was more than oversold. Every seat was occupied. The aisles were covered with GI's standing or sleeping on the floor. My rail ticket, issued at the time my orders were given, seemed out of place. The railroad conductor just went through the motions of taking tickets. We ultimately arrived in St. Louis where we changed trains for Washington DC.

I met some of the Camp Fannin guys and we were on our way together.

Ft. Meade here we come!

Ft. Meade was near the Capitol. Since we arrived in the morning we had four or five hours to spend looking around before reporting at 5:00 p.m. as ordered.

When we went down the empty corridors of the Capitol, a very cordial lady met us "rubber-necking" in the hallway. She asked if we werc lost and when we informed her as to who we were and just "browsing" around. She asked us where we were from and when I told her that "Texas was my home... I learned that she was from Dallas! As we were getting better acquainted, she invited us to visit the office of Vice President Henry Wallace... for whom she worked! Wow! His office was very spacious... with a very large desk... more photographs than you could count on a cabinet just behind his desk. The office was also furnished with a conversational corner... with a

sofa and several lounge chairs, all upholstered in leather. These furnishings were comfortably close to a large coffee table, where plans and documents could be placed for reviewing.

Time was rapidly getting close to our time to report for duty at Ft. Meade... onward to the bus station... we have a destination... somewhere.

## Camp Patrick Henry, Virginia

**Next to the atom bomb creation,** the existence of Camp Patrick Henry was one of WWII hidden secrets from all but the President… or so they thought…

This did not erase the constant warnings for "keeping its existence unknown". You could telephone home but could not tell anyone that you were located at "give me liberty or give me death" *a la* Patrick Henry.

*On the move again*

We finally arrived and settled into "barrack life" again. Quick to learn what the routine would be. My buddy Chet Bowen gave me a preview of the plans to keep us busy without forced marches and exercises all day.

The Bowen plan was to attend the morning "roll-call" and then head for the post exchange, otherwise known as the "PX." A late morning snack while waiting for the theatre to open was a lot better than a five mile walk in the country with a group of guys you don't know.

I must admit that Chet does have great ideas—but—when you question "What will they do to us, if they find us goofing off?"

His response was very calm and certain, "You will not be sent home."

It is easy to see the logic of this argument especially while eating popcorn and waiting for the movie to begin.

Later, after the movie and a cool drink for refreshment, we returned to the barrack just as the tired, thirsty soldiers returned from their day in the country, their question, "Where were you guys?"

We became real good at this until we got orders to go to Hampton Roads for the beginning of foreign travel… to a destination, "somewhere."

# All Aboard

**Our trip to Hampton Roads** was uneventful as most excursions in an Army truck are. There wasn't much in the landscape to write home about. When we arrived at our destination, we were in line to move in an orderly manner, right up to the dock.

The local ladies had arrived with home-made donuts and coffee for those who wanted a refreshment. I was not a coffee man but could not refuse their home-made donuts as a matter of gratitude and for their sincere hospitality.

They looked real good and tasted the same, so much so that I ate two.

As I enjoyed the refreshment, an orderly column of soldiers wearing the same uniforms as the German war prisoners at Camp Fannin, came off of the boat. In fact, they were prisoners from the war in Sicily and you couldn't help but think: "the war was over for them and will begin soon for us."

We boarded the boat and I really was tired and in need of something refreshing. I had been assigned a bunk and took possession at once. Chet was with me and his bunk was nearby.

Also nearby, was a shower room. Boy! I could really use a shower to lift my spirits.

I went immediately into action, disrobed, turned the water on and adjusted the control to the level desired. A large bar of soap was conveniently located and I went into action. Nothing happened. Not one to give up easily, I repeated the process with a lot of determination but the result was the same. I placed the "blame" squarely on the Army purchasing agent who wouldn't dare supply this soap for the officers.

Another soldier entered his shower and I warned him about the lack of success. I was experiencing. lousy soap! His answer was very prompt, "It is not the soap, it is the salt water. It will not produce a lather."

Live and learn.

As I pondered this explanation, the more convinced I became that he was probably right.

I hope the Germans POW's were also denied the lather.

# CHAPTER 5

## This is a Bon Voyage...

**A**t last we are heading out to sea. Traveling without an escort made you wonder if there might be a German submarine just waiting to welcome us as we headed south. As this thought lingered, another more positive alternative entered the race. A much better thought developed that was sending us to Panama, to guard the canal!

Our liberty ship was not exactly "QE2," the deck was not designed to accommodate all of us at the same time. The sleeping accommodations were designed to make us feel "together."

Now, why didn't we think of this in the first place? This really made a lot of sense. This rumor developed so rapidly that some of the more talented GI's started to rumba on deck and sing all of the Latin songs. *"Begin the Beguine"* soon became our favorite!

At sunrise the day following the anticipation of "guarding the canal" ended... when, during the night, our ship had changed course and we were heading due east to join Humphrey Bogart

and Ingrid Bergman in *Casa Blanca. Begin the Beguine* was replaced with *As Time Goes By* and *Play it Again Sam*… Uncle Sam is in charge.

We made it into port but it was announced on loud speaker that we were welcome to Casa Blanca but the town was "off limits" and reservations for us were at the U.S. Army Camp Don B. Passage, named in memory of the first American soldier killed in the North African campaign, November, 1942, or so we were informed.

We marched to our new tent city and were assigned pyramidal tents that would accommodate eight GI's with their duffel bags. We were also advised to be alert to the Arab boys who paid no attention to the fence that bordered the tented area. They were especially aware of the trip adjustments the soldiers needed to make and would be most vulnerable the first night.

They watched our arrival from their side of the fence and spoke fluent English in four letter words letting us know that we were more than welcome and trusted that we would get a good night's sleep.

Guard duty was provided by soldiers who had been at the camp for a week or more. They established a "tent city" with four tents arranged in a large square area while we new arrivals soundly slept on the ground that was covered with GI blankets and our duffel bags became our pillows.

On awakening in the morning, we realized that we had company during the night. In spite of the guard assigned to protect the four occupied tents the Arab youth ignored the guard, silently invaded the tents and all of the noise, if there was any, came from soldiers snoring. The Arab boys would steal what was most desired and available.

For the next few days we went through long difficult marches of several miles each day getting acquainted with the neighborhood and it didn't take long to realize how fortunate we were to be Americans.

These forced marches took their toll. We had been issued combat boots to wear and get accustomed to long marches with new footwear. All of this was fine except my boots were not new. They had been worn a lot and the sole had picked up a nail and transferred it to me. The result: pain from a badly cut right foot that the medic washed with a purple colored medication. They issued me another pair of boots. These were also "pre-owned." My wound did not qualify for a purple heart decoration, only a purple foot.

*Play it again Sam*

All good things come to an end. And thank the Lord, some bad things do too. We were about to leave Camp Don B. Passage and go on the trip of a lifetime.

# The Train Trip that Ripley Wouldn't Believe

**After getting adjusted to life at** Camp Don B. Passage, the Army decided to "treat" us with a train ride. After all my experiences with railroads in Marshall, Texas where I had a very successful career selling newspapers to train travelers for many destinations. We boarded a World War I vintage boxcar. The car with narrow gauge rails was called *40 and 8* in earlier times; capacity: forty men or eight horses by those standards. We had about a dozen men plus a 40/50 gallon lyster bag, with spigot in the center of the car. Each of us was supplied with an army blanket and a supply of K-rations.

There were some shortages, no seats, the floor would serve that purpose. No toilet facility, no Sears catalogue. I wonder how Bill Mauldin the creator of "Willie and Joe," would have handled this situation. In most ways we lacked the basics for a journey anywhere. Much of our trip would be in the Atlas mountains. We began our journey in Casablanca, Morocco and it would end at Oran, Algeria.

We were advised that there would be numerous stops along the way and the Arabs would just appear from out of nowhere. These folks were selling food items… very tempting when you are limited to K-rations.

The army had one order on the Arab menu "if you can't peel it, don't eat it"!

The nights in the Atlas mountains were very chilly. The blanket issued was welcome. Some of the soldiers preferred sleeping "outside" the boxcar on a small platform (with steps) that could accommodate an extra sleeper. This was a very difficult way to spend the night, always on guard.

When the train stopped in the mountain an Arab hand would emerge in the dark and attempt to relieve you of your blanket.

We did, ultimately, make it to Oran. What a contrast. We were not permitted to go into Casablanca and couldn't compare it with Oran. I will always remember Oran with flags from all of the Allied nations hanging along the streets.

We did not go into the countryside at all.

Back on a boat and headed for Naples. We traveled much of the trip at night. We arrived at Messina, Sicily in the dark. No one permitted on deck, no smoking at all. The Germans bombed the harbor of Naples every night.

A tremendous amount of damage that we would see the following day.

# Strike Up the Band

**As we approached Naples** the cost of war became obvious. What really caught my attention was the level of traffic, pedestrian and auto. The people seemed to accept their condition as a permanent fact of life with no reconstruction activity. We were marching through the streets without creating any public awareness of our existence.

We continued moving in file, with duffel bags, until we reached a train depot. Boarding the train that seemed to be waiting, we traveled north to Caserta. I remember it being very different from Naples. It was clean, quiet. and lovely. All of this made sense when I learned that the royal family (House of Savoy) resided here.

All of the above statement was true but what I did not know at that time, was that the Supreme Allied Headquarters was now occupying the Royal Palace.

A short distance away was the "repple-depple" the way GI's describe it. Officially, it is a "replacement depot." This means your next destination would be to a Division that has suffered casualties and needs replacements to fill the vacancies.

On the bright side: Chet Bowen and I were still together.

We were located in an area that had just recently been added to the camp and needed some basic improvements. High on the list was creating a latrine. There were no provisions, such as a covered building with toilets, urinals, lavatories, etc.

None of these existed at the moment so you had to improvise and dig a slit-trench nearby, roughly 24"x 48"x 30" to serve our needs until normal accommodations could be made, that would include toilet paper, hopefully.

It was another "hurry up and wait" situation.

We also learned that each evening, the German Luftwaffe came over with just one aircraft to bomb Naples. We could not see it but the sound was always the same. A very "high in the sky" sound that one could not miss. Those of us "down under" referred to the pilot as "bed check Charlie."

## Bulletin

On May 11 at 2300 hours one of the largest artillery barrages in history began from Cassino to the sea. Six battalions of artillery fired, without interruption, for one hour. We were not on the receiving end of this mammoth barrage and it was hard to believe the enemy would survive but they did and they were waiting for us.

*Artillery barrage–1600 artillery–from Cassino to the sea, 11 hours from 2300*

# It is Hard to Volunteer

**After this historic artillery attack,** Chet said to me, "Raymond, you and I are the only guys still together from the Camp Fannin days. Just the two of us. I hope we can continue this togetherness. Do you have a favorite Division?"

My answer was easy, I would like to be assigned to the 36th Infantry Division. It was the Texas National Guard Division and I would know a lot of the guys from my home town.

Chet thought the choice was proper and since Wyoming did not have a Division, he would like to continue together. He then added "let's go down to the replacement office and volunteer for the 36th."

When we asked to meet with the First Sergeant there was a long pause. Finally, we went into his office, introduced ourselves, and stated our request for assignment together to the 36th Infantry Div.

His visual expression said it all. But just for the record you would have thought "we wanted to go back home" and were here to make this request.

His response went something like this: "*NO!*"

After this carefully considered request, he went on to remind us, that we were in a US Army Infantry replacement center. We would be assigned to meet the requests of a Division in need of replacements for those killed, wounded or captured. Personal requests such as ours would not be considered.

I learned one valuable lesson from this meeting: I would never volunteer again while in the U.S. Army! Never.

# A week to Remember, Malaria & Goumiers

**Shortly after this unsuccessful** assignment request to the 36th Infantry Division, I came down with a very high temperature, 102°. It was feared, at the time, that I had malaria. Another reason for this quick diagnosis was the fact that Italy was known to be ready to share this problem with others not known to me.

It did not make me feel any better to learn that German soldiers were also victims of malaria. The more Germans, the better. The main treatment involved a now discontinued drug—atebrin. One of the possible side effects from atebrin is discoloring.

My stay in the hospital was not without new experiences, the witnessing of life in a field hospital and the dedication of the staff to treat a wide variety of problems. The nurses made you feel like a member the family.

*Santa Maria Infante*

I was about to experience an event that has created a lifelong memory. As we were very near Cassino and the raging battle taking place. The hospital was filled with wounded patients from Cassino and the surrounding area. These were almost entirely American GI's of all ranks. My malaria was about to retreat, thanks to the motherly care of the Army nurses, and I was able to respond to the call for emergency help for a group of badly wounded non-American soldiers. We were informed that these soldiers were attached to the French Expeditionary Army. With French officers, only they could converse with the wounded who were Berber tribesmen from North Africa, Morocco or Algiers. And they were known as "Goums or Goumiers."

They had customs, carefully observed, and the knife around their waists must remain there, regardless. The hospital needed help in transporting these wounded from the ambulances that brought them from the field of battle to the hospital. In short: we were the stretcher bearers.

This whole scene, with the many varieties of wounds reminded me of the movie *Gone with the Wind* and the hospital scene in Atlanta during the Civil War. Amputations were occurring as rapidly as the doctors could make them. You responded to the directions of a medical traffic manager as to where to place the new arrivals. Your focus had to remain on doing your job and let the doctors and nurses do theirs.

I had only one encounter with a wounded "Goum"… in the latrine. He was there in his pajamas with the large knife carried in a belted scabbard around his waist. We observed each other but no attempt was made to get acquainted.

It was rumored they were very effective "night fighters" and could crawl Into the German area without being detected and use their knives to get rid of the enemy. With good reason, the Germans feared them. It was also rumored they were paid a bonus for removing the "ears" from their enemy. Returning to their camp with this evidence and receive the bonus.

They were also feared by outsiders. They were ruthless, not only with the enemy but also private citizens. Italian villages were dominated by these ruthless soldiers and all of the women, young and old, were raped and abused in such a manner that the Allied policy of liberation and freedom was threatened.

After the fall of Rome they disappeared from my world not to be seen in our area again.

**What a Contrast in Life.... All the way from Broadway.**

After the Goumiers, and while in the hospital, those of us who survived their care were rewarded by an unexpected trip to Naples in our pj's and robes for a special show, fresh from Broadway. The show was put together by Irving Berlin, who not only created the show, he was on the stage in person!

In our hospital attire, we were guaranteed the best seats in the house. The opening scene was Irving Berlin in person clad in a World War I uniform. From the stage he introduced some of the "key" musicians in the orchestra pit. Included in the orchestra was one of my favorite players, Johnny Mince, celebrated clarinetist from the Tommy Dorsey orchestra.

My years of reading *Downbeat* magazine made it possible for me to recognize some of the players by name. After the introductions, Irving Berlin sang a World War I song that he had composed, "Oh! How I Hate to Get Up in the Morning." Although his voice was high in pitch, you could have heard a "pin drop." None of this mattered. It belonged to someone who cared enough to bring a company of Broadway stars to entertain the soldiers.

All of this took place in the San Carlos opera house in Naples in 1943.

Picture source: Prologue Magazine 1996, Vol. 28, No. 2

*Irving Berlin*
This Is the Army
*By Laurence Bergreen*
© 1996 by Laurence Bergreen

# Here Today, Gone Tomorrow and Look What Followed You

**When I returned from the hospital** to the replacement center Chet Bowen was gone! Our run of good luck of receiving the same assignments had ended. When I checked for any news about when and where, it was *"Chet who?"* was nowhere on the planet. It makes you think of joining the Navy, you don't get lost on a ship!

I had no idea where Chet had been assigned. I learned after the war that Chat was assigned to the Third Infantry Division. There was no one left that I knew. This was the way of life if you are a replacement.

In the infantry there is very little chance of long term relationships, with tent-mates or fellow soldiers. Infantry officers have a high turnover rate. This is especially true with lower grade officers, platoon leaders, etc. Even though they hide their rank by putting the metal ID bars under their shirt collars they are always exposed to enemy recognition and the turn-over rate was unbelievable.

Tom Johnson's effort to have me transferred to Camp Hulen and play in his band sounded a lot better all of the time !

Suddenly, my name was called and I was ready for assignment with about 40-50 others and was headed by a very solid looking Captain in paratrooper uniform. We were allowed to relax but stay in line.

He quickly introduced himself as Captain so and so. He added that he would be in charge of developing Rangers for very demanding assignments. The exercise program would separate the men from the boys, and on that note, he challenged any one of us, who thought he was a better man to step forward. And the issue would be settled…now!

We thought that Central Casting had sent a John Wayne act-a-like to give us a hard time. The schedule he outlined contained night problems. Every night. The days would be full of "Ranger-ready" training.

# A Moment to Salute a True Hero

**As I remembered** the "pseudo" Ranger training program, that stopped as suddenly as it started, I began to hear about the fate of the real Rangers at Cisterna, Italy. They were organized by Maj. William Darby in 1942. Darby was a West Point graduate and was dedicated to creating a special force modeled after the British Commandos. He was very successful in creating an elite group, second to none, and led them in the landings at North Africa, Sicily, Salerno and later, Anzio.

Darby's men prevailed in all confrontations with the Germans and surrender was not an option unless they exhausted their ammo. When confronted by an enemy that had increased in size by 71,000 extra troops, unknown to Allied intelligence, Darby was reduced to tears when his men required additional ammo that could not be provided.

Without the necessary provisions they were surrounded and captured

I did not witness this but learned of the details after the war.

*Brigadier General William Darby was a great hero.*
*Killed on April 30, 1945 near Lake Garda in the Po Valley region of Italy.*
*(about one week before the war ended)*

*"So I told Company K they'd just have to work out their replacement problem for themselves."*

# Introducing the 88th Infantry Division

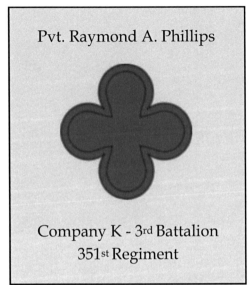

Pvt. Raymond A. Phillips

Company K - 3rd Battalion
351st Regiment

**The 88th Division was activated** on September 4, 1917 at Camp Dodge, Iowa. It was in service during WWI. It served in France from August 1918 to May 1919. The 88th Division was the founder of the American Legion.

The 88th was a reserve Division until July 4, 1942. Camp Gruber, Oklahoma was the designated training center. An excellent maneuver record earned a transfer to Ft. Sam Houston at San Antonio, Texas from Camp Patrick Henry to Casablanca to Oran in WWI vintage box cars (40 and 8). Sound familiar?

The first elements of the 88th entered the front on January 3, 1944.

The full Division was ready for action on February 21, 1944.

On May 15, 1944, approximately, Pvt. Raymond A. Phillips infantry replacement was assigned to Co. K, Third Battalion, 351st Regiment.

A total stranger but ready to go.

# Assignment to the 88th Division – on the Way to Rome

**As previously stated**, I become a rifleman in the 88th Infantry Division, Company K, 3rd Battalion, 351st Regiment. I did not know anyone in the outfit but we soon became engaged with the Germans, south of Rome near a town named Itri. This was the first location by name and I had never heard of it (in fact, I didn't know the names of most of the places encountered).

The Germans valued it and did not want to abandon the area until around the end of May when they moved north of Rome.

We stayed on the front until June 13 and then we went in to a period of restoration near Albano just south of Rome.

Although it is a long line of soldiers, it is just my introduction to the terrain of the future. I will discover that Italy is one mountain followed by more of the same—almost all the way to Austria.

It can, and will get worse—in the northern Apennines.

# Getting Acquainted

**Among my earliest days of** my becoming a rifleman with Co. K we were gathered in a high spot, up in the mountains…

At the time… this whole area was called the Gustav Line. How and when it got its name, I don't know.

Everything was new to me… including my comrades. We had arrived at high spot in the mountains and it was getting colder. We were told that some hot coffee was on the way and that we should enjoy it because the next coffee break would be sometime later. I had never had a taste—much less a cup—of coffee. This was not the case of those around me. One soldier in particular, was really loud in expressing his opinion. I did not know him, but I wanted to be "accepted" so when he turned to me for my opinion of the coffee, I could be honest in telling him, "It is the worst coffee I have ever tasted."

I really don't remember sleeping that night and by daybreak we were ready to continue the movement north.

*"Ya know, I ain't worth a dern in th' morning without a hot cuppa coffee."*

78

I have no recollection of food but we probably had a K-ration for breakfast.

I remember being thirsty by mid-morning. It happened that a stream was nearby and I had a canteen that needed more water. By this time, we were within sniper range so I lay down on my stomach and crawled to the stream to fill my canteen and hoped the water was fresh. You could never be sure but the army had issued a little white pill that would purify the water.

It did the job and I was ready to continue. A few hours later... still no Germans.

We came upon a farmhouse that seemed to be abandoned. Someone fluent in the German language ordered the occupants of the house to come outside — weapons removed — they were in great danger. There was no response so we fired a healthy round from our combined rifles... no response. Carefully, we approached the dwelling only to find it empty... almost.

The occupants were farmers and they had been caught in the middle of the conflict. The Germans had come and gone. They were preparing to eat when we arrived. They didn't invite us to eat but had left a generous lunch. The oven was full of bread, just ready to eat... and we were ready for it. We couldn't be sure if this might be a trap so the captain set up guard detail.

There was a soup with some meat included. That didn't get neglected. I took a generous piece of the bread that was in the size of a large loaf. I made a small loaf and removed a lot of the center. It created an empty bun that I filled with the meat. The result was a king-size sandwich. It was as close to home-made as you would find.

After the feast we continued the pursuit on a full stomach.

We were moving out of this area into an area that prepared us to resume movements north. It was dark and dangerous. If not careful you could walk "off" the mountain.

For security we held the belt of the GI in front and just hoped he would not make a bad move.

The day came for me to see what 16 weeks at Camp Fannin had accomplished. I had become a full-fledged private in Company K, Third Battalion.

They had unleashed their deadly 88mm artillery guns in our direction. When the incoming shells got close to us, we hit the ground. This upset our sergeant, whom I did not know—yet—and he started yelling "getup—we are not going to be pinned down." His orders were followed by "kicking ass" as fast as he could.

This got the attention of all. As we continued to move forward, I noticed that some of the new guys were "shedding" themselves of extra weight—including grenades—I thought of gathering these items for extra weapons for myself. I did tell them to stop—they may need these in the near future. I could not believe anyone would do this.

As we proceeded north, we started seeing the effect our mortars and artillery had on the landscape. Dead cattle in the pastures… dead German soldiers in their summer uniforms, short pants, lightweight and more comfortable than our all wool winter wear.

However—the kraut clothing was not bullet nor shrapnel proof.

# On the Outskirts of Rome

**We were moving** northward but the Germans didn't want to make taking Rome too easy. The fight continued right up to the city limits and then we moved in. The 88th Division was the first Allied Division in Rome and the Italians overwhelmed our arrival, tossing flowers in the sky, opening untold bottles of vino, and hugging and kissing the GI's in a great celebration. The date was June 4 , 1944.

Two days later, June 6, 1944, two momentous events took place. First, I celebrated birthday #19. Second, the Allies landed in Normandy and made all of the headlines.

The war in Italy was relegated to the back page of most newspapers.

*"Th' hell this ain't th' most important hole in th' world. I'm in it."*

## Historical footnote

Since the earlier than anticipated entrance into Rome, two events happened:

Event 1 – It was the first time — ever — that Rome had been invaded from the south.

Event 2 – It has been claimed that American General Mark Clark violated the master plan for the Allied Armies to "encircle the German forces in Italy by directing the American 5th Army to the northeast and meet the British 8th Army directed to the west — completing encirclement this would force the Germans to surrender. Or be destroyed.

Clark chose to head directly for Rome — and glory!

# Welcome Secretary of War Henry L. Stimson and General Mark Clark

**Shortly after Rome,** the 351st Regiment, 88th Infantry Division was ready for the guest of honor, Secretary Stimson, who traveled to Italy for a full inspection of our unit. This special event took place at Tarquinia in the Anzio beachhead area. The secretary was very proud of our achievements and reminded us that the people "back home" were very proud of our victories over the enemy. He went on endlessly to remind us that the Germans were on the run and in the near future we would meet the enemy again and triumph as our country expected.

We were very quiet and attentive to his remarks and thought for a moment, that he should resign his position as Secretary of War and join with us and share the glorious future he could foresee. ("That will be the day"... to quote John Wayne)

*Secretary of War Henry L. Stimson inspects the 311st at Tarquinia*

I recently attended a special book event for a favorite writer of World War II. Not his personal experiences, but for the overall historical events.

I have read most if not all of his books.

I keep his book on the war in Sicily and Italy close at hand—and refer to them often.

However, I have always been puzzled by his lack of coverage of the war in Italy after the fall of Rome on June 4, 1944. Recently, I had the opportunity to ask him why he had stopped writing about the war in Italy soon after Rome—when there was still so much war to come.

His response was not comforting and certainly made me full of doubt that he and I were talking about the same war. The writer explained that he had spent approximately 576 pages on Sicily and Italy—and after June 6, 1944—the main events were taking place in Normandy.

*"Must be a tough objective. Th' old man says we're gonna have th' honor of liberatin' it."*

# The Germans Tried Everything but Nothing Worked for Long

**They were very good** in making war in Italy.

First, they had the Italian landscape on their side. From the northern top to the southern base—the Apennines are almost continuous mountains, there are small valleys, like the Liri, in the south and the Po in the north. Everything else is mountainous.

In addition to the natural barriers, the enemy used "forced labor" to construct defensive safety nets, such as "pill" boxes in many locations, and reinforcing larger cave-like chambers, where groups of soldiers could occupy with heavier weapons—machine guns—and larger supplies of ammunition.

They were in constant defensive preparation in order to meet the Allied armies that stayed in constant pursuit. The Germans also made the most from buildings destroyed by the Allies, the massive amounts of "rubble" that once were buildings, became defensive positions that protected the occupants from the advancing enemy—meaning me and my buddies. This terrain put limits on the use of tanks except as artillery. Gen. George Patton would not be in his element in the war of movement. It was "Willie and Joe" country… as illustrated by the man who knew them best.

*A German Gothic Line defensive position*

*"K Comp'ny artillery commander speakin'."*

# Onwards and Upwards to Volterra

**We had to stay in pursuit of the Krauts.** We found ourselves in a wooded valley with a narrow trail winding its way upwards.

Across from us — some 30 yards — were some GIs from another company. They had some wounded but still had a sense of humor about the predicament they — and now us — were involved in.

They were "cheering us on" and expressing concern for us as we were advancing and they were sidelined with wounded, etc.

In retrospect, it seems strange but it was done with good intentions. They were yelling "go get 'em boys" and how much they were concerned about our welfare and so forth.

There were no Krauts nearby — they had moved out of this ancient town — from Etruscan times. We did not know this at that time — nor particularly interested — but townspeople started meeting us on the upward trail — with *vino* and bread; *vino* and cheese; *vino, vino, vino*. Since I did not drink *vino* and wasn't especially hungry after the big meal earlier — we were more interested in what was ahead. The church towers were the place to be concerned with. The Germans frequently left a sniper in the tower which could be a problem.

I did not speak Italian but I knew enough to ask *Dove i tedesche?* Translated: *Where are the Germans?* We managed to reach Volterra and found it to be "vacated" by the Germans — and so far, we were "all present and accounted for."

# We Discovered Oil Near Volterra

**A German 88mm artillery crew** wanted us and we had a lot of respect for their ability to make life miserable—especially the squad of "Company K" soldiers, so we did all we could to protect ourselves.

We found refuge in the only place available—a small settlement of Tuscan farmhouses that were grouped together—all were solid stone buildings with tile roofs—made to take some of the power of the German 88mm artillery—but not for long.

We took refuge in the basement of one of the houses and found a collection of very large urns that had been filled with olive oil. Some—not all—were completely destroyed—resulting in a pool of olive oil about two or three inches deep. The Kraut artillery moved on to other targets. We got out with feet all "soaked" but ready to leave the oil discovery that saved us for another day.

## Fried chicken, anyone?

One of the guys spotted a yard full of chickens as we entered Volterra.

Apparently, he had been raised on a farm, and knew how to steal a chicken, wring the neck, pluck the feathers, and clean and prepare the chicken for a meal "fit for for king," but not a GI.

After cleaning and preparing—he cooked the chicken in his helmet (without the liner) filling it with water brought to a broil.

The whole process took most of an hour. He was generous with his offer to share freshly cooked chicken with the guys—not for me. Before

the end of the day, the downside of this meal brought on dysentery of major proportions.

"Foxhole Phillips" would not share a "foxhole" with "chicken-eaters" for several days.

The menu read, "Chicken a la helmet."

# It's Hard to "Fool" a Mother

**My mother did not have** a clue as to the activities of the infantry. Or so I thought. When we were at the front, it was not possible to write letters. And so I tried changing the dates, making them frequent so as to project the notion that I had lots of free time and out of harm's way. Or so I thought. Mom was a very good correspondent as you see by the addressed envelope. Plus, she included a pocket Bible, complete with metal cover. Just in case. Or so she thought, I know she prayed for me and with divine intervention, we were a formidable pair—mother and son.

So we knew.

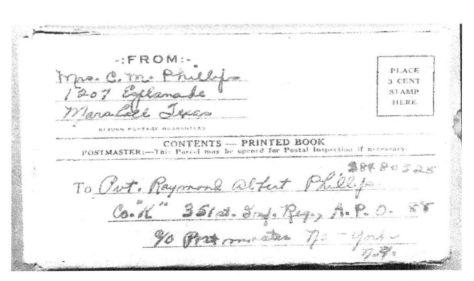

# From the Frying Pan — into the Fire

**After Volterra, we continued the pursuit** of the Germans. The sergeant ordered "fix bayonets." If that doesn't get your attention nothing will. The Germans had become more determined to stop the advances made since Volterra. We found ourselves in a wheat field that had recently been mowed and there was no place for concealment. We were pretty exposed to enemy fire and it started coming from all directions and the "German-88" artillery weapon was so accurate that we felt the Germans would really cause major problems.

This was west of Montecatini. I was "hugging" the ground and couldn't find any other way to protect myself without cover. Then, our artillery returned the German fire and really changed the scene. I can remember the arrival of our tanks and this was an unusual event. The terrain in Italy is not designed for vigorous tank activity. (General Patton would have been frustrated by the limited use of tanks.)

At one point, I found myself alongside a tank and realized this was not a good location. I thought this "friendly" tank would attract a lot of German fire and I did not care to be included.

*I'll let ya' know if I find th' one wot invented the 88.*

This battle started on July 9 and ended on July 13. There were times when I wondered how my mother would receive the news, if things didn't work out. The German advantage of terrain ultimately was overcome as we brought in our tanks and artillery, plus a lot of rifle company power to settle the issue.

Elements of the 34th and 91st Divisions were joining the battle and this additional force really made us equal to the German forces. A German panzer grenadier regiment was virtually destroyed. My regiment, the 351st Infantry, lost 80 killed and over 300 wounded. The Germans losses were approximately 250 killed and 425 prisoners taken and a large supply of German weapons. The battle is known as the Battle at Laiatico.* Our battalion received a Presidential Unit Citation.

We were relieved from the front line and returned to the Volterra area to begin training for the next campaign.

Divine intervention had saved my life and would again, in the near future.

* The tenor Andrea Bocceli is a native of Laiatico.

The President of The United States, Franklin D. Roosevelt, cited the Third Battalion of the 351st Infantry Regiment for its remarkable and outstanding fighting in the battle of LAIATICO. The citation follows:

'THE 3rd BATTALION, 351st INFANTRY REGIMENT, is cited for outstanding performance of duty in action, during the period 9 to 13 July 1944, in the vicinity of Laiatico, Italy. During the attack on strongly fortified German positions in the vicinity of Laiatico the 3rd BATTALION occupied an advanced position, devoid of cover and with both flanks exposed, and for three days withstood heavy enemy artillery and mortar bombardments as well as three vicious enemy counterattacks supported by tanks. Displaying courage, skill and determined fighting spirit, the battalion frustrated all enemy efforts to defend the town and surrounding strategic positions. On the fourth day, the 3rd BATTALION launched a night attack and penetrated the German stronghold from the flanks and rear. Aggressively exploiting its breakthrough, the battalion seized a German regimental command post after a savage hand-to-hand struggle in the darkness and cut the main escape route from the Laiatico hill mass. As a result of the 3RD BATTALION'S prodigious efforts, 425 prisoners were taken, 250 Germans were killed or wounded, and a large quantity of enemy weapons were captured which were promptly employed with telling effect against the battered German forces. The timely capture of this key enemy defensive position compelled the Germans to abandon a carefully prepared, strongly defended line and opened the route of advance to the Arno River. The fearlessness, heroic determination, and aggressive fighting spirit of the officers and men of the 3rd BATTALION, 351st INFANTRY REGIMENT resulted in a performance which brings honor to the Armed Forces of the United States.'

*The Third Battalion earned a Presidential Unit Citation for the remarkable and outstanding fighting at Laiatico, Italy.*
*July 9-13, 1944*

# After Laiatico My World is about to Change

**Our company was located near Volterra** and began training for our next campaign in the northern Apennines. We were living in "pup tents," two men in each of the small tents. My tent-mate was a young soldier from Paterson, New Jersey.

For the life of me, I can't recall his name (which is the case more often now) but I do remember how much he suffered from killing two Germans at Laiatico. I tried to help him move on from this situation… but… I had no success. Finally, I reminded him that he could not be sure that he killed them for… when you are involved in maximum firing at a targeted area, you cannot be sure that you hit anything you were just one of several soldiers firing. He did not buy this idea… so… I told him that he was making it hard on himself and could make bad decisions in future engagements if he couldn't "move on"and deal with "the now" and not "the past."

He was killed in the northern Apennines in September 1944.

I am getting ahead of my story about training for what would be known as "The Gothic Line."

Along with several others, we had a "free" day and wanted to get away from the Army routine. With this in mind, we went to Volterra close by and just started sightseeing, without worrying about the war.

The town was full of friendly activity complete with a local photographer who worked the sidewalks to persuade GIs to send a photo home… presto!

He caught me in a good mood complete with the combat infantryman badge that I had just been awarded.

I began hearing music… American Jazz… somewhere nearby. My buddies were not into searching for the music source… they had other things on there minds.

I continued the search as the sound got louder and louder. Bingo! Here I am standing outside of this building that was jam packed with US military of all ranks. The musicians were all GIs playing everything I knew and loved… American-style jazz.

I worked my way to where the music-makers were playing and got acquainted with them. Finally, one of the guys asked if I played a horn. I told them I played the trombone before being drafted. To this he responded, "We have one nearby." And before you could spell "trombone," bingo, again a trombone was magically brought from the back and handed to me.

There was no time to warm-up you just started playing!

It had been almost a year since I put my trombone aside and put on a uniform. Who cares? Now is now, so live it up, while you can!

This went on for about an hour and the crowd never left. All ranks were present and enjoying every moment. Finally, in unison, the musicians had to stop… and go back to their units.

And so it went…one of the most memorable days of my life.

**Details**

*Height: 6' 1.5"*
*Weight: 165 lbs*
*Hair: Brown (GI cut)*
*Complexion: Basic Marshall, Texas with*
*    Italian sun*
*Clothing: GI style, all seasons*
*Extra attachment: newly awarded*
*    combat infantryman badge*

# Time to Move Up in the Apennines

**The time came for us to remove the tents**, get back in the trucks and head for the mountains. We finally arrived at some unknown spot, tired, chilly, and hungry. We did not have long to wait. For a jeep loaded with hot food and maybe, just maybe, some mail!

The driver unloaded the large container loaded with hot food and he had a stack of mail, plus an envelope for Pvt. Raymond Phillips. I was called to report to the driver who informed me that I was to return with him. What? Where? Why?

He told me to get into the jeep because he had many things to do at headquarters. I refused to get in the jeep without the captain's ok. Captain Marks was no longer our CO but his replacement, Captain Richart was summoned and read the document concerning me.

All he said was: "Phillips you are to return with the driver."

Why?

Captain Richart replied: "I don't know, but you are to return with the driver.

When we arrived at headquarters I learned that I had been transferred to the 88th Division band. (Tom Johnson finally prevailed?)

I later learned that Warrant Officer Alex D. Menz, Director of the 88th Division band, had been in the audience in Volterra when I played with the small jazz combo—and he needed another trombone player.

Divine Intervention strikes again.

# CHAPTER 6

## Montecatini, What a Place to Rest, and you never know who will "show"

Montecatini is about 40 km from Florence and was a popular destination for the well-healed European for their mineral waters—like the American Saratoga Springs or the Hot Springs. Arkansas.

(It has also claimed to be the birthplace of Pinocchio.)

Because of the many hotels, it became a hospital center for the wounded German soldiers. All of the rooftops of the numerous hotels had a red cross painted to ward off Allied bombing.

When the 88th Division removed the Germans following the Battle at Laiatico they made a different use of its facilities. The place was ideal for the division to use as a recreation center when its troops came off the front line. U.S. Army special services set up a permanent unit to entertain the GI's. This company had their own musicians, comedians, and a very talented soldier who performed special aerial gymnastic exhibitions and did a comedy routine titled "Sad Sack and the Sergeant."

*R & R in Montecatini*

*"In most ways it's better than a foxhole"*

This very athletic soldier became the sergeant and a very small GI with an ill fitted uniform was, of course, Sad Sack.

Each time we came off the front for a rest, I would return to this theatre for a good evening. Many months later, when I returned home, and discharged, a recent edition of *Life* magazine had on its cover, the photo of a new film star. It really caught my attention and I hurriedly turned the pages to read the article and guess what? It was the GI from Montecatini who was the sergeant in the Army shows… and his name was Burt Lancaster.

*Lilly (Virginia Christine), the Swede (Burt Lancaster) and Kitty (Ava Gardner)*

# A Surprise Discovery Nearby

**After the 88th Division** took over Montecatini it became the primary R & R center for other Allied troops, as well.

Although I was somewhat familiar with the environs... we were off the line in Montecatini on a leisurely tour of the outskirts and not prepared for what we encountered in the nearby hills.

There were four or five of us and suddenly we came upon a German machine gun nest.

There were four or five Kraut soldiers — dead at their firing positions — sitting down but ready for action. They seemed eager to take us by surprise. They achieved the surprise — but not the way planned.

Each soldier had been killed — and fully attired, with helmets on, and seated on the ground in firing positions. Shrapnel had penetrated their helmets.

On closer inspection, it was apparent that a mortar or artillery or both had hit its target. It appeared that death had been sudden.

Their bodies were not yet decomposed and looked like figures in a Madam Tussaud Wax Museum in London.

I was curious about this unexpected discovery but unlike some of my buddies, I had no interest in closer inspection. I reminded them of the possible, though unlikely, "booby trap" devices on their bodies. This did not deter the more curious who expected to find something of value and to "heck" with any planted "decoys." One found a letter in the pocket of one soldier in German, it remained unread.

One of my comrades discovered some "blue steel" razor blades in the pocket of one soldier and jokingly gave them to me with the promise of a "lifetime" of quality shaves.

That was a safe prediction for someone 19 years old and shaved once every week.

**A Moment to Pause and Remember the Past**

**During my freshman year** at Southwestern University, one of the ministerial students living in Mood Hall was a young fellow from San Antonio, named Don Box who later became the minister at the First Methodist Church in Gladewater, Texas. Don had a delightful sense of humor—more than expected for a preacher (Don was not the "Elmer Gantry" type-in any way).

As I approached the age of 18—and the draft—Don always referred to me as "Foxhole" Phillips... all the while smiling because, being a ministerial student, he was not subject to military service (nor was he likely to share a "foxhole" with anyone.

Somehow, I knew that Don was right in predicting my future. I took some comfort in the following:

> There are only two ways to live your life. One is as though nothing is a miracle. The other is as though everything is a miracle.
>
> Albert Einstein

## A New Assignment—complete with foxholes

**I was ordered to guard the division** duffel bags in a stable at a race track near Montecatini.

How in the world I arrived at this location, I could not believe.

What does this assignment have to do with the band?

This "duffel bag" assignment would not last long.

I learned, for the first time, that the band members served as POW guards, when the division was on the front line. I also learned that the guard locations were different. Some guards were located at the front to be available when POW's were first captured. We lived in foxholes and were exposed to all enemy fire. The POWs were removed... *ASAP*... and taken under guard to be interrogated in a rear area.

Living in a foxhole in the bitter cold of the northern Apennines would require warm, dry socks and clothing. I also took a copy of the *Stars and Stripes* newspaper and inserted it in between my shirt and body. It proved to be "warmer" than Mother Nature.

Whatever works!

*En route to nighttime patrol in the Northern Apennines*

We wore reversible top-coats with a hood, all in white, to blend in with the foxholes. One night, I heard the sound of movement quite near my foxhole. I was certain it was a German patrol. I prepared my M1 rifle to challenge the intruders when I discovered it was an American patrol, returning from a survey of the German position.

It scared me no end when I realized how close I came to firing on friends.

> Lord,
> help me to remember that nothing
> is going to happen to me today that
> you and I together can't handle.
> Amen

# The Buckle Issue

**During the war,** I observed the belt buckles of the German soldiers with a lot of curiosity. On each buckle was inscribed *Gott mit uns.* In English it means *God is with us.*

I found this to be puzzling. I could not understand how anyone who saw the atrocities committed by the Germans would ever believe that God would approve of these actions.

All of this led me to question my own survival. I do know that "divine intervention" and "divine guidance" were a profound influence on my life, and saved it on numerous occasions. One has only to remember how and when the transfer to the 88th Division band occurred, without any request or effort on my part, and how many transfer requests Tom Johnson had made, to have me transferred to the Camp Hulen band, without success.

It was a "non issue" for whatever reason. I would not personally request or pursue a transfer. If or when it came, I knew that God was with me, with or without a buckle.

# Introducing Some of our Principal Adversaries

**The commander of all German forces** in Italy was Field Marshal Albert Kesselring. He had been a prominent military leader from the beginning of World War II—he was an outstanding officer and highly decorated.

Kesselring—also known as "Smiling Albert"—was very aware of the significant German loses in Italy and wanted to slow down Allied advance… and destroy our forces in the Apennines….

He was injured in a car accident in October and replaced by General Heinrich von Vietinghoff, who would remain in command of all German forces in Italy for the remainder of the war. Another leading German officer was Major General Karl Lothar-Schultz. General Schultz was in charge of the extraordinary 1st Parachute Division.

The 1st Parachute Division was highly regarded for its very long history—from Crete to Russia to Italy and the battles with the 88th "Blue Devils." At the end of the war Schultz told his interrogators that "the 88th Division is the best we have fought against."

Some called the German 1st Parachute Division the "Green Devils."

The fourth general in the line-up is Gen. Karl Wolff whose mentor was Heinrich Himmler—the brutal founder & chief of the German Schutzstaffein—or German SS. Gen. Karl Wolff was the commander of all SS forces in Italy. He was not only very close to Himmler he was also a favorite of Adolph Hitler.

(Gen. Wolff was the only German General encountered by me—as you will learn later.)

Field Marshall
Albert Kesserling

Karl Wolff, SS Commander

Colonel General Heinrich
von Vietinghoff

General
Karl Lothar Schulz

# And a Few Heroes: Colonel Charles P. Furr, 1918–1944

**I was just an eighteen year old** private trained to be a replacement and assigned to the 88th Infantry Division.

The 88th was a very aggressive division and when assigned to K Company I had a lot to learn… and very little time. My basic training of 16 weeks at Camp Fannin was really inadequate… and so was the pay.

I was in good physical condition… but… still a private. The Private First Class—or PFC—would come shortly with a pay raise.

I had really learned from my comrades—as we "looked out for each other."

You learn more by observation—watching what others do, who are more experienced… and have survived.

One thing I knew… as did my comrades… I wanted to do my best and not be a burden on them.

This was not just my attitude… it was shared by all of us.

I was very fortunate to have Itri, Rome, Volterra, Laiatico behind me. Plus, an untold number of places that remain unknown.

I felt sorry for the new officers…the 2nd lieutenants in particular, who always wanted to perform well—but couldn't… because many didn't survive very long.

There was, however one officer that I will always remember. He was the Commander of the Third Battalion, 351st Regiment. I knew his name as Major (soon to be Lt. Colonel) Charles P. Furr from Rock Hill, South Carolina.

He would go anywhere to keep moving forward… he carried his pistol into troubled areas—right alongside his men—giving the Germans the problem of dealing with such a courageous leader.

Until recently, I thought him to be a West Point graduate.

No one could come out of the private sector, at his age, and teach themselves how to effectively command a battalion—or so I thought. His leadership skills always took him to the scene of the action. He led by example. I pity the adversary who stood in his way… I was advised that he was wounded on the way to Rome… and it didn't stop him.

I was very aware of him at Laiatico where he led our battalion to victory and our battalion received a Presidential Citation.

# An Eye Witness Report on the Tragic Loss of Lieutenant Colonel Charles P. Furr

**The nights of September 24 and 25,** 1944 will long be remembered by the fighting men of the 351st Infantry by the savage windstorm that lashed at them as they huddled behind rocks for protection from a sixty mile an hour gale. In the howling, driving wind it was impossible to hear the shells scream in, and the courageous mule skinners took their losses and brought up food and ammunition.

The Third Battalion jumped off at 0300 hours with Company K leading, followed by Companies M and L. Lt. Col. Furr led his battalion along the side of a ridge which joined the German-held ridge line at right angles... roughly shaped like a letter "T." The Germans allowed the screening platoon to pass through their positions and then opened fire on the remainder of Company K with from 6 to 8 machine guns at point blank range... inflicting terrific casualties on the company.

Colonel Furr who was leading the column, plunged into the close-quarters fighting, killing several Germans with his pistol.

While gallantly leading his men, Colonel Furr lost his life and the 351st Infantry lost one of the most promising and fearless young commanders in the Army.

---

Private Rickenbacker of Company K provided this eyewitness report as it appeared in the history of the 351st Infantry Regiment in World War II.

# A place of honor

**It has come to pass** that the citizens of Castel del Rio — in the Apennines, have placed a bronze plaque to commemorate the sacrifice of Col. Charles P. Furr and the men of K Company, 351st Regiment, 88th Infantry Division, U.S. 5th Army — on September 24, 1944.

The monument is located near the spot where Col. Furr was killed. Also found near Col. Furr's body, a coin dated 1875 that was returned to Jay Trimmer — who in turn sent it to Col. Furr's daughter, Sandra Furr Hannon of Rock Hill, South Carolina.

*Monument to Lt. Col. Charles P. Furr who fell here September 25, 1944. Photo credit: TracesofWar.com; Photo: Aiazzi Fabio*

*Lt. Col. Charles P. Furr*

# Jay D. Trimmer, POW 0068766

**I met Jay Trimmer through Fred Lincoln,** who is president of the 88th Division Veterans Association. In fact, I have called Fred so often that he probably thinks I have "verbal dysentery." Fred gave me Jay's telephone number and so began an 88th Division reunion almost 70 years after the war.

It turned out that Jay was also in K Company which became my first assignment in the 88th. It may be hard to believe that I did not know Jay in K Company but it is true.

An infantry company has about 180 members. Jay, was a member of K Company of the 88th Division during an early training period.

When I contacted Jay by telephone, he was very generous with his information about Col. Charles P. Furr and had been near the site but did not witness this loss.

In fact, Jay was taken prisoner and spent the rest of the war as POW 0068766. When Jay was liberated he weighed 75 pounds! Jay shared his story with me about his life after the war. And his involvement with the monument dedicated to Col. Furr and the men who fought and died at Castel del Rio.

# CHAPTER 7

## After the Tough Beginning—It Stays Tough

After the severe losses in September and October, mother nature has decided to make it tougher and colder. The northern Apennines have introduced a new and more difficult element... cold, rain, ice, wind... in daily doses... even my old "foxhole" has become a more uncomfortable address. Hot food, coffee, etc. is not on the menu. K-rations are welcome—frozen or not.

Patrols—by either side—are few, but not abandoned.

Another unexpected element has presented itself in the form of a bridge—no name—in need of guarding.

## As the Winter Continued

**We did everything** we could to get warm and stay warm.

A new dimension was added to the situation.

The big battle going on in Northern Europe.(now known as the Battle of the Bulge) changed our routine. Would it spread to Italy? Our leaders were very sensitive to the threat of a possible German offensive in our area, in concert with the one in Belgium.

If this did happen, the bridge was the only way to transport heavy weapons (tanks, artillery, trucks, etc.).

It was decided to prepare for the destruction of the bridge should it become useful to the enemy. Engineers planted explosives on our side of the gorge and instructed us in their detonation.

Very near the bridge was an abandoned house made of stone. It also had a very large fireplace and a good supply of wood.

Wow!

Our orders were simple: guard the bridge* and destroy it, if necessary. Two men would remain at the bridge in shifts, two hours on and four hours off. There were six of us. Four shifts each pair, until the threat retreated after a week or ten days.

---

* The bridge near the town of Castel Del Rio seems to be a survivor—after all the care and protection, including the price of pleurisy incurred by those of us on guard—research has indicated it was constructed circa 1500 AD—and— is the only bridge able to support traffic.

I have never been so cold in my life.

Two hours of that cold was as much as you could endure. I have no idea what the temperature was but it was very cold. Your whole being was frozen–stiff! Getting into the jeep after two hours of guard duty, was very difficult.

For the time being, we were not guarding POW's and that was a great relief.

The large room of the farmhouse was made of stone and timber. The fireplace was the better part of one wall and also had a good supply of wood.

The furniture for seating must have been placed elsewhere. We didn't miss it.

The floor was a welcome location for us to stretch out and get some rest in between shifts. The stone walls might protect us from Kraut 88mm artillery should they decide to shell us for being close to their neighborhood.

After a period of time I developed pleurisy.

Pleurisy liked me so much it came home with me after the war.

*Sacked in*

# There's No Business Like *Snow* Business

**As the hard winter continued** the front line is fairly static. Patrols by the Germans and patrols by our side are the main activities… but… they were not the only activities.

There is no limit to the marketing of the world's oldest profession.

A very entrepreneurial Italian civilian, a pimp, accompanied by an attractive young female (all females were attractive to GIs) had set up shop near a "safe" cave that offered a somewhat level of "protection" from the war.

Believe it or not they were not successful in their marketing effort with the GI's. (I am reasonably sure that they worked the German side also while the front was quiet and "peaceful.")

(I often wondered if you took advantage of their service and were wounded, while in the act, would you still receive a Purple Heart medal?)

While the front was static a better use of time was sweeping for enemy mines.

*Mine sweeps*

# Goodbye Apennines, Hello Po Valley

**After the winter months** in the mountains spring finally arrived and the Po Valley campaign got under way. Out of the mountains and into this huge valley, we could undertake a war of fluid troop and tank movement, a rare strategy for the war in Italy.

So fluid, in fact, it was hard to know where the front was. For once, we were traveling by truck and passing miles of German equipment, abandoned for lack of gasoline. Vehicles of all kinds, trucks, jeeps, tanks, they were lining each side of the road for miles. We found another, old stone villa to use as a POW compound where we could collect Germans who were conceding in ever-increasing numbers in some areas and not at all, in others.

After moving into the villa, we learned that it had served as a headquarters for the German 1st Parachute Division, our old nemesis. It was full with loads of records, maps, and personal items.

I was never one to collect souvenirs I just wanted to "get on with it" and go home.

Included among the documents was an unusual book detailing the largest parachute drop in German military history, the parachute invasion of Crete in May, 1942 employed 15,000 paratroopers and of these more than 7,000 were killed.

Hitler was shocked at the size of the loss and vowed to never use paratroop jumping assignments again. Instead, they would be used as elite ground infantry.

This book came home with me as another reminder of those times.

*The one shown above appears to be the compound serving as the German 1st Parachute Division headquarters.*

*Kreta - Sieg tkr Kuhnsten The only souvenir I came home with. Many years later, I had a special box made for the souvenir. The spine is shown above.*

Prisoners in the Po Valley

*German Helmet*
*Swastika Decal*

*German soldiers were surrendering by the hundreds*
*and were placed under guard in the largest*
*compounds available.*

## The End of the War is in Sight — and so is the hair-splitting

**The war was reaching its end,** confusion reigned supreme everywhere in the Po Valley. There were areas of continued conflict where life was short for those who refused to lay down their arms. We were ordered to continue to move up the Brenner Pass as if we were going to Austria. After several miles of truck-travel a jeep overtook us and signaled us off the road to park in the yard of a farmer.

"Do any of you guys speak German?"

A GI from Iowa replied in German, enough to satisfy their needs. This delay gave us enough time to wash as well as we could but not as much as we needed. I didn't spend any time trying to shave since I really didn't need one. I made the mistake of trying to wash my hair with GI soap and as I dried the hair and started the combing process… Guess what? My scalp was a victim of the Italian campaign. It didn't like my company anymore and wanted to leave my head.

You win some—you lose some.

(Over time, you lose even more.)

After a couple of hours, our buddy from Iowa returned by jeep. We were curious about his errand… and then he said, "It's over."

"What do you mean 'it's over.'"

Again he said, "The war is over."

# At Last—"It's Over"

**The war ended in Italy, May 2, 1945.**

The war in the Apennines was very costly to our side.

The writer James Holland whose book *Italy's Sorrow* had this to say: "The Gothic Line battles had seen some of the fiercest fighting and the worst conditions of the entire Italian campaign."

He goes on to say that the casualties in September and October were higher than at any point in the campaign—worse even than those at Cassino.

The 88th Division lost an appalling 9,167 of the full strength of around 9,250 infantrymen. Over 5,000 were battle casualties, the rest due to illness and combat fatigue.

I continued my service in the 88th Division until the end of the Italian campaign... participating in the following: Rome, Arno, January 22 to September 9, 1944; North Apennines, September 10 to April 4,1945; Po Valley, April 5 to May 2,1945.

# On to Bolzano

**As the war settled down** I found myself on guard duty at the headquarters of the German SS in Italy.

General Karl Wolff was in command of all German SS forces in Italy… I remember him well as we guarded him and members of the SS headquarters staff in Bolzano, Italy.

On the day of our arrival Col. J. C. Fry with a squad of armed guards went to the residence of Gen. Wolff with a war-

*SS Headquarters, Berlin*

*Karl Wolff, SS Commander*

rant for his arrest. As it happened, Mrs. Wolff met Col. Fry at the door with a loud protest for this "uncalled act of intrusion."

The General was enjoying his birthday dinner with an impressive list of guests—including Gen. Vietinghoff. Madam Wolff threatened Col Fry and his squad with protests to higher authority.

Col. Fry took her into custody, as well.

We were permitted to converse with members and some could speak English as well as we could.

One young SS soldier wanted to buy a carton of American cigarettes, it so happened that I had a carton and traded it for a German camera with Ziess-Ikon lens. I was not a camera "buff" but my sister Myrtle would really enjoy taking pictures with this fine camera.

The SS soldier told me that he could take me to hiding places for items of great value—if I would permit him to lead me there my response was quick and final: "You are not leaving this room. Save your information about hidden wealth until you are interrogated. I will advise our authorities of your willingness to cooperate."

Two days later, our guard squad was given new orders away from the SS headquarters. We went to a large barn in the country some 5 or 10 miles away from the SS building.

The barn contained 12 or 15 German females. Our orders were to be strictly observed. Do not attempt, in any manner, to fraternize with these women.

We did not understand their crying. It was constant.

One could easily attribute their behavior to the fear of being raped.

Where? How? And most importantly… Why?

There was nothing appealing about most if any of them. I concluded that they were grieving the fact—Germany had lost the war and they did not know what their future would be. We were not "gloating" or celebrating. We were outside of the barn and had "zero" interest going inside.

Thank goodness, this detail didn't last but a day or two.

As the day went by, I noticed a man—some 50 yards away—walking towards us at a pretty fast pace. As he got closer, he reached into a coat pocket and removed an envelope. For some reason, I looked "receptive" to him and he unfolded a letter from Detroit, Michigan—in English.

The letter was from a relative in Detroit.

He wanted to know if I might know him? (Is he serious?)

And—if so—would I translate the letter from English to Italian. (Believe me... this is true... who could make this up?)

I told him I was from Texas—hundreds of miles from Detroit and—I could not translate the letter .

I couldn't help feeling sorry for him.

(I'm now 90 years old but I still remember the plight of this old man.)


**A Tragic Truck Ride...**

**The incident I remember most** was in the rear of a US Army truck, loaded with displaced civilians. There were four GI's on each truck. Two in the cab and two in the back of the truck. We were ordered to carry weapons since there were still pockets of danger with Germans of unending resistance. We were transporting the civilians to a larger collection area, where they would be included in the enormous task of returning them to their homelands They had been removed from their homes and made part of a workforce, at the mercy of the Germans. They performed all kinds of labor for the Nazis, always under the fear of punishment or death.

Included in our truck was a young woman, maybe 16 years young. I could tell that she didn't know how to behave and to survive this soldier with a gun (meaning me). I could sense that she had experienced abuse and terror at the hands of "soldiers with guns." I readily discovered that she was unable to express herself in English...I realized that she thought that men wanted only "one thing"... and she would not

be able to provide this "requirement." Since the language barrier made it impossible for her to communicate this "shortcoming" she did not want me to hurt her. She raised her skirt to show me why she could not provide the expected service — this was her "monthly period."

I was barely 19, and did not know very much about such things.

I just felt sorry for her and what she has had to endure.

I trust that Divine Guidance returned her to her home and family.

## Pleasure follows Pain

**I was in the hospital again**. This time I was in the ancient town of Pistoia in Tuscany near Florence.

When I recovered enough to receive a pass for the day, I went with friends to Florence. I had never been to this historic city. We were taking it in and suddenly we stopped in front of a cafe that reminded me of home. First of all, there were cafe curtains "shirred" at the top and left the upper half of the window completely free—uncovered.

They reminded me of the treatment at the Ginnachio hotel/restaurant in Marshall, Texas—where I sold newspapers to train travelers when I was 8 or 10 years old.

Another unexpected treatment was the menu in the window, above the shirred curtains.

Automatically, the message was "come in and have a meal with us." We responded promptly and once inside this heavenly cafe had tabletops covered with linen. We found table for four, complete with napkins, also in linen, to match the table covers. It sure did beat K-rations in a box.

My mother could have prepared the menu… everything explained in "English" of all things. It did not require standing in line with a "mess-kit"

Divine Guidance had taken us to a heavenly eatery… even though "bread pudding" was not on the menu.

It was affordable. It was delicious.

The host in charge was the Salvation Army.

# Strike Up the Band and Slow Down the Horse

**Shortly after the Bolzano duty**, the division band was assembled for a return to musical activities — living in a vacant mansion on Lake Garda.

We had all of the amenities the previous weeks of guarding POW's had lacked, we could play volley ball, tennis, or swim in a world class lake.

We had rehearsal time for "good-will" concerts in the nearby villages... near Bolzano — with the Alps in the background.

Army life had really changed for the better.

Nearby, the US Army had discovered a stable with horses for GI's to ride. When the band guys learned this they were filled with added excitement. The "foxhole days" were over.

As a group we went forward to the stable to visit with the Italian stable manager and make arrangements to ride... and select the horses to ride. I dreaded every minute of this — my denial of riding experience — was met with real doubt.

I was accused of "false modesty."

On the side — and out of my hearing range — I was "singled out" and described to the stable manager as being from Texas — the American west where cowboys in the movies live — and ride.

Therefore — I should be provided with a "spirited horse."

And I was given a horse so spirited that it did not like the company of the other horses—and would speed ahead of the others to avoid their company.

He didn't care much for me either and speedily ran close to the tree hoping to get rid of me.

This was really getting out of hand. The command *"whoa"* didn't mean anything in Italian. The only thing left for me was *"aspetta un momento."*

I just knew that this life would not last long—and it didn't. The US Army had a new & different plan for my musical future.

All kinds of rumors began and we had no idea what lay ahead.

Were we going to be part of the occupation? Are we going home and more training for assignment to the Pacific? No one really knew—but—out of the blue, some, including me, were transferred to a completely different unit… that would play for officer clubs. Traveling U.S.O. shows if they needed musicians.

We were commonly referred to as the 5th Army Special Service Orchestra.

# CHAPTER 8

## Will Clare Boothe Luce Help Us Strike Up the Band?

Some amongst us had impressive "big band" careers with the likes of Artie Shaw, Gene Krupa and the Hit Parade Orchestra.

There was, however, a storm brewing over the lack of good musical instruments. It seems that the war years had taken their toll on the condition of the U.S. government band instruments. However, there was a "magic moment" in the form of Clare Boothe Luce, a highly gifted American celebrity widely known for her patriotic activities and who would be visiting Italy in the near future. Like next week.

Some wise guy considered this to be a "golden opportunity" to enlist the support of Mrs. Luce in using her influence to help us retire our old, war-weary, band instruments. And replace them with new instruments.

Being a young, naive band member (who privately considered this a dumb idea), I let my name be among the others placed in a hat drawn in the presence of all and *bingo*, guess whose name was drawn?

Our appeal was expressed on a sheet of paper, to be presented personally by yours truly to Madame Luce, who always seemed to be in the company of high ranking brass. Well, the time came, I proudly

presented our appeal in a new, unused envelope with a few words of gratitude for her help in this matter.

Did she open the envelope? Did she read our plea? This will go down in history as one of the few failures in US military history.

(The least they could have done was to send me home immediately as a "war-weary veteran.")

# Travel Agent Supreme None Other than the Army of the United States

**If you have ever dreamed of taking** the trip of your life I can recommend a travel agency that can provide this service. In most cases, you do not pay a fee for their services. For example, during WWII they provided a "cost free" trip from Marshall, Texas to selected North African spots and sunny-rainy-icy-snowy-cold-hot… Italy.

After the war, the trip of a lifetime was planned by the US Army in association with the Swiss government. This time the trip was based entirely on the number of "points" each soldier had acquired during the war. This was not a problem for me for I had a lot of points.

The trip choices were: Venice, Nice, and Switzerland. A"no brainer" for me

The soldiers eligible for this trip were to meet in Milan, become acquainted, and receive their room-mate assignments for the trip of one week to Lugano, Bern, Lucerne, Zurich and everything in between.

My roommate assignment was Ken Okamoto from the 442nd Nisei Regiment, Japanese-American Infantry. When you couldn't get Chet Bowen, this was a good alternative. I will make you acquainted, shortly, with the one and only Ken Okamoto and his historic comrades.

## Trip menu

Trip payment (rail, hotel, 2 meals daily: $250 paid with Allied Military currency) — in advance — was not a problem.

Maximum currency allowance per person—$150 Allied Military currency for "walking around money." Doesn't sound like much but when all basics have been paid in advance it can all be spent buying my "dream wrist watch."

(I wanted to purchase a thin watch. It must be "superthin." I had noticed that all of the captured German officers wore very thick watches with all sorts of multiple sweeping hands and I wanted to "go thin" in my selection. I found it in Zurich on the first day and spent my total allowance. And I still have it. It was made by Omega and is about the size of a quarter. And thin-thin-thin. It is joy to look at—all in gold— everything I dreamed owning.)

**Back to the Trip**

This payment covered all hotel accommodations, two meals per day plus all train travel throughout Switzerland. The Swiss were concerned with the possible inflation that would result from the rich American soldiers invading their fragile economy. Really?

This is where I met a group of Japanese-American GI's—known as Nisei. Most were from Hawaii but some came from California.

The Nisei soldiers were all volunteers in the Army.

The U.S. government was so concerned with large number of Japanese in the country, after Pearl Harbor, they were placed in internment camps, mainly in California. Young men could avoid this process if they volunteered for U.S. military service.

A special unit, the 442nd Infantry Regiment, was created and it became the most highly decorated unit in American military history. The conservative Swiss were overcome with curiosity about these soldiers in American military uniforms in the company of American soldiers.

The Nisei soldiers brought their ukuleles with them and performed native songs and dances in the nightclubs we attended. They wore "make-believe hula skirts," by wrapping Eisenhower jackets around the waist backwards so the sleeves were tied in the back… very clever and convincing.

When they played their ukuleles and sang and danced it was more than the conservative Swiss could absorb.

My roommate, Ken Okamoto was one of the most cheerful individuals on the planet and could have won elective office in ultra-conservative Switzerland.

# Hollywood Discovers Ken Okamoto

**In 1951, while employed** by the New York department store B. Altman & Company, I "took" an afternoon off to go to the Capitol Theatre. The world premier movie "Go for Broke," starring Van Johnson, was being shown.

I arrived and settled in my seat with a bag of "popcorn" as the showing got underway.

As the movie began, it took very little time for me to see my traveling friend and sometime roommate — Ken Okamoto!

After the first run, I went backstage and the fun began.

Ken was surprised to see an old friend from the Italian/Swiss days.

This was our last re-union.

(On the occasion of writing my first book *The Journey* I tried, for weeks, seeking to find Ken Okamoto — only to be told by a Nisei veteran that the name "Okamoto" was as common as "Smith or Jones" in their culture.)

*I went to the premier showing in New York in 1951 and had a brief reunion with Ken, who was in the film.*

## Farewell to the Troops

**A farewell party** the night before my departure for home on December 17 (from Naples) was held at the non-com's club in Livorno (Leghorn).

I had a major concern and here it is: I never had an alcoholic drink in my life, never, truthfully. I did not want to be a "party-poop" so I decided to have my first beer. I had heard that GI beer was not the "real deal," that it was much lighter than regular beer and the only kind available at the club.

Seated close to our table for eight was a GI that must have been at the club all day. This "unknown soldier" was really "loaded and loud." He was alone but did not want to remain "alone." We made no effort to include him in our group. He was not deterred by our ignoring his determination to join us. His persistence went forward by informing us of his origins in this manner.

"I am from the most beautiful state in the United States."

No response.

"I am from the most beautiful county in the most beautiful state in the United States."

No response.

To continue his ranting he stepped up a notch:

"I am from the most beautiful city, in the most beautiful county, in the most beautiful state in the United States."

By this time, he was so "worked up" that he dared to tap my shoulder and personally confront me with the question:

"Do you know what and where these locales are?"

Finally, I had enough of his "loaded" intrusion of my party. So I replied in a calm, cool manner:

"Yes, the answers to all of your intrusive questions in their order of inquiry: you are referring to the state of Texas, Harrison County, City of Marshall. Now leave us alone."

He was stunned by my answers because they were all true. It took him a while to absorb all of my answers because they were unexpected but to make it more unbelievable, he was Perry Harkins from Marshall, Texas and worked in the First National Bank that was owned by the Key family that includes my dear friend Mimi Key.

I better get home soon, all of these events are heavy and hard to carry.

By the way, on July 22, 2014 at 5:00 p.m. Raymond A. Phillips and Mary Key (still known as Mimi) were married at the Church of the Incarnation (Episcopal) on McKinney Avenue, Dallas, Texas. Officiated by Bishop Anthony Burton.

## I'm Going Home. Merry Christmas for Sure!

**I had finally accumulated** the required number of "points necessary" to return home and be honorably discharged.

I took the train from Livorno (Leghorn) to Rome. It had been a long time since my last visit. It was good to revisit "the eternal city" and I made the most of sight-seeing — and selling a carton of cigarettes for some "walking around" money. (it helped replenish some of the "damage" the wrist watch cost.)

Whatever works.

After a couple of days in Rome we went on to Naples and boarded an aircraft carrier. The USS Randolph — that had been converted into a troop ship!

The Randolph would carry 7,500 GI's to New York in about 7 days!

All things being equal.

*USS Randolph. Photo courtesy of www.navsource.org.*

Somehow, the Army knew that a group of musicians would be on board — although we were strangers to each other. They made us a deal: if we would provide music for the GIs during meal time — we could eat first — and — have a private "stateroom" to relax during the day — and — play the inventory of "V" discs on hand and read a supply of books, etc. (they did not have the proper equipment on board, to play the discs on a large sound system for all aboard… I am glad that we were needed.)

The "V" discs were much larger than ordinary 78 rpm at home. This size was used in radio stations to broadcast an extended program, with commercials, etc. On the radio.

Another treat—I had not heard any American big band music by big name bands in a very long time… Les Brown orchestra and especially the new Woody Herman band with the likes of bassist Chubby Jackson, "Flip" Phillips on sax (no relation) and a new (for me) jazz trombonist named Bill Harris.

We were destined to arrive in New York City in less than 7 days! (if everything went smoothly)

Indeed, everything was going well in the Mediterranean. It was like a big lake. When we entered the Atlantic we hit an 80 mile per hour gale that demonstrated the power—and danger of the ocean, the flight deck was off limits. Everything on the flight deck was either removed or secured with very heavy cables.

The hanger deck was home to the 7,500 soldiers—a good many were involved in a dice game for the entire trip. A GI Blanket was spread over the floor location and stayed in place until we reached Staten Island.

There were several such locations and they were not bothered by the weather. After what seemed like an eternity—the storm went away.

In addition, the flight deck became safe again…

As we moved steadily westward one could see two towers above the clouds. New Yorkers on board identified them as the Empire State and Chrysler buildings

I finally made it to New York!

More and more of Long Island became recognizable to the natives on board. The USS Randolph was now in New York harbor—in a reserved location. On Staten Island. Just waiting for us to arrive.

It was also time for Santa clause to arrive—and he did!

A fleet of ferryboats took us on board for a trip across the harbor—so close to the Statue of Liberty—I felt as if I could touch her.

As we passed this lovely lady, a look on our right side revealed a lighted Manhattan aglow with Christmas cheer.

We finally made it to New Jersey—to Fort Dix—and almost immediately, we transferred to a special troop train.

I had never seen the likes of this train—it had no seats. Each car was furnished with bunk beds—securely anchored at the floor and at the top.

It was very comfortable—you could view the passing landscape lying down or sitting up.

But this was just the beginning. The train left New Jersey and headed north east, at first.

It was Christmas Eve and as the train changed course, we were headed across "Norman Rockwell America" or so it appeared. I was so captivated by the small towns we passed in the night—each decorated with Christmas lights. One after the other, we traveled without stopping in Ohio, Indiana, Illinois—each all dressed with Christmas lights and snow on the ground.

And I expected to see Santa Claus at any moment. I did not sleep a wink. The whole scene was too good to be true. I did, however, slip off during the evening glory and when the morning light awakened me, the train had turned a corner and the course of travel was to the southwest.

I saw a sign that told me we were in Arkansas and headed to familiar country. Believe it or not, I had made a complete circle in my Army life and as the train came to a stop... we were in Camp Fannin, Texas... where it all began.

Hollywood would not dare to tell a story so unlikely to happen.

I hold the distinct honor of being at Camp Fannin when it first opened—and to return when it was being closed, I received my discharge on December 31, 1945.

Happy New Year—the war is over—and our side won!

## Mr & Mrs. C. M. Phillips Proudly Present

the Phillips Family response to Pearl Harbor from the beginning to the end

My sister, **Myrtle Phillips Wyche**, lived in Gladewater, Texas with husband Everette M. Wyche. Myrtle served all of her brothers and their comrades, with boxes of candy, shaving supplies, etc. throughout the war. She was the pride of Company K. In many ways, she was our secret weapon.

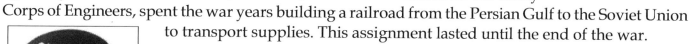

My brother, **Clifford A. Phillips,** was a special apprentice with the Texas & Pacific Railroad waiting for an appointment to West Point through the office of Texas Congressman, Wright Patman.

While serving in the machine shop, the tips of two fingers were severed— "good-bye West Point." He did, however, earn a commission in the Army Corps of Engineers, spent the war years building a railroad from the Persian Gulf to the Soviet Union to transport supplies. This assignment lasted until the end of the war.

(For the record: as the war progressed, many male friends of C. A. Phillips were in the service, some overseas, and some of the Marshall mothers could not understand why "that Phillips boy" was still a "civilian." When C. A. "got wind of this" he was deeply upset… to the extent, he sent a telegram to U.S. Chief of Staff General George Marshall requesting that Lt. Clifford A. Phillips be called to active duty—effective immediately—if not sooner.)

This request was accepted at once with orders to report to Camp Claiborne, Louisiana.)

My second brother, **Richard E. Phillips,** wanted to become a pilot in the U.S. Air Corps. A grammar school football injury caused a hernia and his application to air training to be denied—unless he corrected the problem, surgically—at his expense.

This did not happen—he later served in the U.S. Navy—stationed in Brazil, never aboard a ship, at sea until the end of the war. He came home with a lovely Brazilian wife—Hanniete Ramalho Phillips.

**Raymond A. Phillips** was in high school on Pearl Harbor day. He wanted to play the trombone in a big band, instead, when he was 18 he was drafted into the Army with service in North Africa and Italy. He was there long enough to earn the following: the Combat Infantryman Badge, a Good Conduct Medal, a WWII Victory Medal, a Presidential Unit Citation, Army of Occupation Medal-Bronze Star Medal, African Middle-Eastern campaign with three Bronze Stars, and a honorable discharge with a note of "thanks" from the local draft board (friends & neighbors) who sent him on a pre-paid journey overseas and home on December 31, 1945.

Happy New Year.

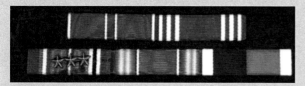

*Two rows of ribbons*

*Combat Infantryman Badge*

*Good Conduct Medal*

*Army Occupation Medal*

*Bronze Star Medal*

*African Middle Eastern Campaign with Three Bronze Stars*

*World War II Victory Medal*

*Presidential Unit Citation*

  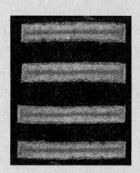

*Shoulder Patches (left to right): 88th Infantry Division, Fifth Army, Two Years of Service*

# Honorable Discharge... (with some surprises)

**On December 31, 1945**, I was so happy to be home that I had not taken the time to read the details of my Army service record. At age twenty — I was ready to get on with my life — time was really passing quickly and I needed to "catch up".

When I finally got around to reading about my discharge. I discovered that I had been in units that were new to me — name wise — 117th Army Ground Forces band — bandsman trombone (it was formed after the war and commonly recognized as the 5th Army Special Service Orchestra.)

It went on to say that I earned a Combat Infantryman Badge on August 15, 1944 — true — not even close to just "being in a band."

What is the "point " in revealing these discrepancies after 71 years.?

Nothing, really. They just bring out the "Willie & Joe" of (Bill Mauldin fame) — in me.

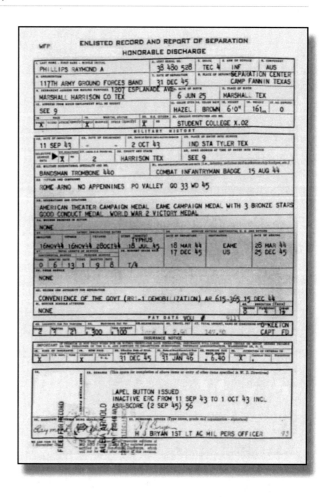

The Phillips family– as others across the country–made a family contribution.

# The End is Here

The interruption of our fraternity meeting—on December 7, 1941 at Perman Grundy's home in Marshall, Texas completely set in play the years of world change yet—I am still here. What a journey it has been...

Before going forward, it is time to pay tribute to those who did not make it back home to Marshall from the war years.

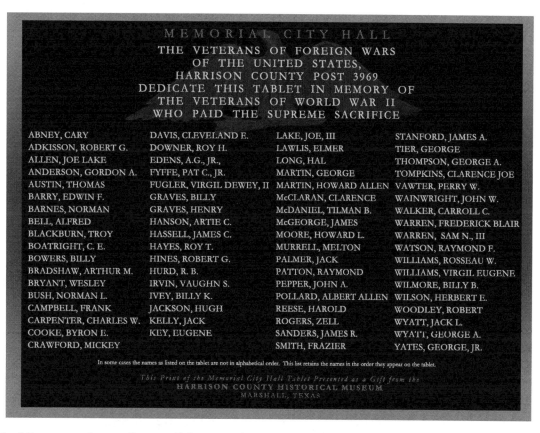

MEMORIAL CITY HALL

THE VETERANS OF FOREIGN WARS
OF THE UNITED STATES,
HARRISON COUNTY POST 3969
DEDICATE THIS TABLET IN MEMORY OF
THE VETERANS OF WORLD WAR II
WHO PAID THE SUPREME SACRIFICE

ABNEY, CARY
ADKISSON, ROBERT G.
ALLEN, JOE LAKE
ANDERSON, GORDON A.
AUSTIN, THOMAS
BARRY, EDWIN F.
BARNES, NORMAN
BELL, ALFRED
BLACKBURN, TROY
BOATRIGHT, C. E.
BOWERS, BILLY
BRADSHAW, ARTHUR M.
BRYANT, WESLEY
BUSH, NORMAN L.
CAMPBELL, FRANK
CARPENTER, CHARLES W.
COOKE, BYRON E.
CRAWFORD, MICKEY

DAVIS, CLEVELAND E.
DOWNER, ROY H.
EDENS, A.G., JR.,
FYFFE, PAT C., JR.,
FUGLER, VIRGIL DEWEY, II
GRAVES, BILLY
GRAVES, HENRY
HANSON, ARTIE C.
HASSELL, JAMES C.
HAYES, ROY T.
HINES, ROBERT G.
HURD, R. B.
IRVIN, VAUGHN S.
IVEY, BILLY K.
JACKSON, HUGH
KELLY, JACK
KEY, EUGENE

LAKE, JOE, III
LAWLIS, ELMER
LONG, HAL
MARTIN, GEORGE
MARTIN, HOWARD ALLEN
McCLARAN, CLARENCE
McDANIEL, TILMAN B.
McGEORGE, JAMES
MOORE, HOWARD L.
MURRELL, MELTON
PALMER, JACK
PATTON, RAYMOND
PEPPER, JOHN A.
POLLARD, ALBERT ALLEN
REESE, HAROLD
ROGERS, ZELL
SANDERS, JAMES R.
SMITH, FRAZIER

STANFORD, JAMES A.
TIER, GEORGE
THOMPSON, GEORGE A.
TOMPKINS, CLARENCE JOE
VAWTER, PERRY W.
WAINWRIGHT, JOHN W.
WALKER, CARROLL C.
WARREN, FREDERICK BLAIR
WARREN, SAM N., III
WATSON, RAYMOND F.
WILLIAMS, ROSSEAU W.
WILLIAMS, VIRGIL EUGENE
WILMORE, BILLY B.
WILSON, HERBERT E.
WOODLEY, ROBERT
WYATT, JACK L.
WYATT, GEORGE A.
YATES, GEORGE, JR.

In some cases the names as listed on the tablet are not in alphabetical order. This list retains the names in the order they appear on the tablet.

This Print of the Memorial City Hall Tablet Presented as a Gift from the
HARRISON COUNTY HISTORICAL MUSEUM
MARSHALL, TEXAS

Their names are recorded here, and our flag will honor their service forever.

Now that the war in Italy is over and I have returned home safely, I have time to reflect on my varied experiences in a country that suffered so much in the war but retains its historic beauty.

Bill Mauldin says it best—on the final page:

*Beautiful view. Is there one for the enlisted men?*